Praise for *Gender-Inclusive Schools:*
How to Affirm and Support Gender-Expansive Students

"As a transgender educator who has known and worked with Dave Edwards for seven years, I wholeheartedly endorse his book. Dave combines practical and accessible strategies with a passionate personal connection as a parent of a gender-expansive child. This invaluable resource equips educators with essential tools to support and affirm gender-diverse students, offering model language and reflective activities to foster truly inclusive learning environments." —**Mitchell Klages-Bombich, M.S.Ed.,** professional development coordinator, United Federation of Teachers Positive Learning Collaborative

"As an educator, a teacher of teachers, and a parent, I have gained so much wisdom and so many inclusive strategies and tools from Dave Edwards. His message is clear, kind, practical, and powerful. If you work with children in any capacity, you should have this book in your possession. It might even help you save a child's life." —**Shanie Israel, M.Ed.,** associate director of curriculum, professional development, and multicultural innovation, Montclair Kimberley Academy, Montclair, New Jersey

"As a pediatrician, I see the outsized mental health impact that schools have on gender-expansive children, for better or worse. When a school community approaches *all* its students with intention, love, and a sense of duty, these children blossom and thrive. Schools that embrace the concepts so thoughtfully organized and articulated here by Dave Edwards will be doing more for their students' mental health than all of us medical providers combined." —**Rhamy Magid, M.D.,** pediatric hospitalist at Children's Minnesota, former medical director of Hennepin Healthcare's Pediatric Gender and Sexual Health Clinic

"This book is a resource that every educator, no matter their role, should possess, study, and use to move the needle of school climate toward affirmation, inclusion, celebration, and safety." —**Toni Smith,** board member and professional development lead, Georgia Safe Schools Coalition

"Every student deserves the opportunity to learn, and it is the responsibility of the adults in their lives to create safe and supportive environments for them to do so. In this necessary book, Dave Edwards offers resources and implementable strategies to ensure that school leadership has effective tools to create and maintain affirming learning communities for gender-expansive students." —**Martinique Starnes, Ed.D.,** director of diversity, equity, inclusion, and justice, Westside Neighborhood School, Los Angeles, California

"In *Gender-Inclusive Schools*, Dave Edwards shares a wealth of knowledge from his years of work with educators across the country. This accessible guide is a great foundation for anyone seeking to create schools that are welcoming and inclusive of LGBTQ+ students—not just on paper, but in practice." —**Kat Rohn,** executive director, OutFront Minnesota

"This essential guide for educators is an invaluable resource for fostering inclusivity and acceptance in the classroom. Its exceptional organization ensures it will be a go-to tool for implementing inclusive practices, making it indispensable for supporting all students. Dave Edwards's experience shines through every page." —**Lourdes Buck, M.A.,** coordinator of educational equity, Saint Vrain Valley Schools, Longmont, Colorado, and author of *Sue's Sky*

"Dave Edwards's approach is clear and practical, helping schools ground their practices and communication in their school's mission so that everyone in the community can understand this work. The tools in this book will help educators support the kind of environment we want for all of our students: to be known in the ways they choose, to have appropriate privacy and confidentiality, and to be fully included and able to participate in all aspects of school life."—**Julie Strong, Ph.D.,** assistant head of school for teaching and learning, French American International School and International High School, San Francisco, California

"*Gender-Inclusive Schools* is an invaluable resource for educators and school staff, offering practical strategies and insights to support transgender and gender-expansive students. It's an essential tool that I highly recommend for creating inclusive classrooms. Educators often fear making mistakes. While there's no way to get it right every time, this book empowers educators and school staff to commit to doing better consistently, using real-life examples heard in classrooms all the time." —**Rebby Kern,** training lead, Human Rights Campaign Foundation's Welcoming Schools

"Dave Edwards has written the essential guide for ensuring that gender-expansive students are safe and supported in school. Guided by two principles—supporting happy, healthy kids and respecting their privacy and confidentiality—this book offers practical and accessible steps for educators working to ensure safe and supportive schools. The book relies on the wealth of experience Dave has as a parent, educator, and leader in this work." —**Danielle Murray, M.Ed.,** assistant head of school, Boston Latin School, Boston, Massachusetts

"Dave Edwards facilitates productive discussions, helping us address underlying concerns, clarify misconceptions, and develop clear communication strategies for use in classrooms and with parents. This book is going to be incredibly informative and helpful for our educators." —**Gretchen Ievers, M.S.,** assistant head of primary school, Montclair Kimberley Academy, Montclair, New Jersey

"Gender in education has been a topic of debate since humans first created institutions for learning, and it has once again come to the forefront of conversation. This book provides answers to questions on the minds of countless families, educators, and administrators about how to best create an environment where a person of any gender can learn and grow free of stigma and discrimination. The book provides concrete examples and strategies that can be employed today to prepare our youth for a more interconnected and gender-affirming future." —**Rick Oculto, M.S.W.,** education specialist

"I was honored to represent Dave Edwards and his family when they brought a precedent-setting case to end discrimination at his daughter's school—and I agree with him: There's no need for educators to wait for legal rulings to get it right. If you are an educator, now is the time for you to take action on behalf of gender-expansive students in your school. In ten deeply researched and eminently practical chapters, this book will show you how." —**Jill Gaulding,** cofounder of Gender Justice

"Dave Edwards has created a blueprint for other parents, educators, and helping professionals. His invaluable direct experience is laid out in this tremendous resource." —**Andrea Jenkins,** transgender advocate, author, poet, and Minneapolis city councilmember

"This guidebook will prove to be a vital resource for anyone who wants to do better by our young people. Students in our schools deserve nothing less than to be safe, secure, valued and loved—so they can grow, learn, and thrive. As an out LGBTQ+ legislator, I receive frequent calls from parents, teachers, and administrators in every corner of Minnesota wanting help responding to challenges their LGBTQ+ students and families are facing. Sometimes those challenges are grave and dire. I always turn to Dave Edwards for help. I'm so glad others will have access through this book to his wisdom and insights." —**Scott Dibble,** Minnesota state senator

Gender Inclusive Schools

How to **Affirm** and **Support** Gender-Expansive Students

Dave Edwards

Foreword by Kade Goepferd, M.D.

free spirit
PUBLISHING®

Library of Congress Cataloging-in-Publication Data

Names: Edwards, David, 1985- author.

Title: Gender-inclusive schools : how to affirm and support gender-expansive students / David Edwards.

Description: Minneapolis, MN : Free Spirit Publishing, [2025] | Includes bibliographical references.

Identifiers: LCCN 2023058486 (print) | LCCN 2023058487 (ebook) | ISBN 9798885543965 (paperback) | ISBN 9798885543989 (ebook) | ISBN 9798885544009 (epub)

Subjects: LCSH: Gender identity in education--United States. | Sex differences in education--United States. | Educational equalization--United States. | Sexual minority students--Civil rights--United States. | Discrimination in education--United States--Prevention.

Classification: LCC LC212.92 .E39 2025 (print) | LCC LC212.92 (ebook) | DDC 371.8210973--dc23/eng/20240508

LC record available at https://lccn.loc.gov/2023058486

LC ebook record available at https://lccn.loc.gov/2023058487

Free Spirit Publishing does not have control over or assume responsibility for author or third-party websites and their content. At the time of this book's publication, all facts and figures cited within are the most current available. All telephone numbers, addresses, and website URLs are accurate and active; all publications, organizations, websites, and other resources exist as described in this book; and all have been verified as of February 2024. If you find an error or believe that a resource listed here is not as described, please contact Free Spirit Publishing.

Edited by Christine Zuchora-Walske

Cover and interior design by Mayfly book design

Printed by: 70548

Printed in: China

PO#: 12369

Free Spirit Publishing

An imprint of Teacher Created Materials

9850 51st Avenue North, Suite 100

Minneapolis, MN 55442

(612) 338-2068

help4kids@freespirit.com

freespirit.com

Dedication

To my amazing older daughter, Hildie: I am so lucky to be in your orbit as you courageously, unapologetically, and authentically create a better world with your brilliant light and power. You have forever changed our family for the better by being exactly who you are supposed to be. Keep being you.

To my outstanding younger daughter, Dahlia: You fill our family with love and laughter. I am in awe of the way you lead and influence every space you are in with your bravery, kindness, humor, and resolve. Keep being you.

To my forever partner and wife, Hannah: Parenting with you has been the biggest responsibility and privilege of both of our lives. It's been more eventful than I could have imagined, but our love for each other has always been effortless. Your work to support gender-expansive kids and their families is inspiring to me and the world. Thank you for truly seeing me and for being my biggest supporter. We make an amazing team.

To transgender, nonbinary, and gender-expansive students learning in every school and in every community all over the world: You are worthy of respect, affirmation, and love. You are perfect.

Contents

Foreword

by Kade Goepferd, M.D.

I have wanted to be a pediatrician since I was a kid. I knew this was my life's calling once I got to college and learned the powerful impact that access to essential health care has on a child's ability to thrive and become a strong, happy, and healthy adult.

I've been in pediatrics for twenty years now, but it didn't take me long to learn that my best efforts go only so far. Most of what impacts a child's overall health and well-being happens beyond the walls of my exam room. In the United States, only about 20 percent of a person's overall health outcomes are linked to clinical care. The remaining 80 percent of health outcomes are driven by environmental factors (UW Population Health Institute 2024). And as both a pediatrician and a parent, I am acutely aware of how much time children spend in school environments and how profoundly school shapes their experience of life.

As a pediatrician who cares for transgender and gender-diverse youth, I have heard countless stories about their school environments, from unsafe bathroom and locker room experiences to health issues from avoiding bathrooms or being unable to access gender-neutral bathrooms in school. Most of my patients have experienced gender-based harassment or bullying in their schools—some of it so severe that they had to change schools, move to online education, or homeschool. A poll by the Trevor Project found that 39 percent of LGBTQ+ young people seriously considered attempting suicide in the past year, including 46 percent of transgender and nonbinary young people. LGBTQ+ youth of color reported higher rates than their White peers (Nath et al. 2024).

While numbers like this are disheartening, the good news is that 54 percent of transgender and nonbinary young people found their school to be gender-affirming, and those youth reported lower rates of attempting suicide (Nath et al. 2024). When anti-transgender policies and political agendas don't prevent them from thriving, trans and nonbinary kids have access to many protective factors at school—supportive teachers, supportive school counselors, and peer support through sports teams and other activities.

If you are an educator, a school counselor, a school administrator, or anyone else impacting school climate and environment, this book is for you. Your efforts may sometimes feel like trying to boil the ocean. But know that even small changes are important. For example, using a child's correct personal pronouns that align with their gender identity reduces symptoms of depression and suicidal ideation and behavior. You *can* make a difference.

This book matters. I believe the strategies and tools within are invaluable resources for all who shape educational environments. They could literally be lifesaving for LGBTQ+ young people.

Thank you to Dave Edwards for writing this important book to help all school community members create safer, more supportive, and more gender-inclusive school environments. I can't be effective at helping transgender and gender-diverse kids thrive unless they are also supported in their schools.

And thank you to you, reader, for caring about the health and well-being of all students. By reading this book, you are taking a crucial step toward improving the lives of transgender and gender-diverse students in your community.

References

Nath, R., D. D. Matthews, J. P. DeChants, S. Hobaica, C. M. Clark, A. B. Taylor, and G. Muñoz. 2024. 2024 US National Survey on the Mental Health of LGBTQ+ Young People. West Hollywood, California: The Trevor Project. thetrevorproject.org/survey-2024.

UW Population Health Institute. 2024. "Health Outcomes." *County Health Rankings and Roadmaps*. countyhealthrankings.org/health-data/health-outcomes.

Introduction

My child, Hildie, was in kindergarten when she first experienced bullying and discrimination for being transgender. In fall 2015, our family had requested that, as part of an anti-bullying lesson, classes read *My Princess Boy*, a picture book about gender-expansive kids, to help them understand Hildie's gender expression. The ensuing events confronted us with a reality we hadn't previously understood: many people would refuse to accept our child for being her authentic self.

Administrators at Nova Classical Academy, a public K–12 charter school in Saint Paul, Minnesota, emailed the whole school community about the lesson. A hostile and vocal group of parents then began a months-long crusade to prevent the acceptance and inclusion of gender-expansive students. School board meetings turned into circuses, with hundreds of parents making hate-filled public comments, petitions, and testimony laced with anti-trans propaganda. Alliance Defending Freedom, an international organization identified by the Southern Poverty Law Center as a hate group, held a rally in the school gymnasium. Websites such as The Daily Signal, The Federalist, and many conspiracy blogs published our home address and job histories to encourage threats against our family.

All of this happened because of a simple request meant to help a kindergartner feel safe, welcome, and included in her school.

After months of fighting, Nova's board chair and attorney decided that no discussions about LGBTQ+ topics could take place at school without parents and caregivers first being invited to opt out of the information. In short, staff couldn't respond to the daily bullying and hate speech directed at our five-year-old without half her classmates walking out of the room at their parents' request.

When Nova made it clear they would not support our family or protect our daughter, we decided to switch schools. In spring 2016, we found a location where we knew our child could be safe—an option not available to every family. We filed a human rights complaint with the city, who found probable cause that Nova had discriminated against our minor child because of her gender identity. Following this finding, we agreed to a settlement to avoid a lengthy lawsuit and to focus on productive steps toward making sure our child, and the many children like her, could attend school without fear of discrimination.

Why I Wrote This Book

The 2015–2016 school year was a watershed for me and my family, but there's a lot more to our story too. Here are a few other important things to know about us and our advocacy work and why I wrote this book.

I am a queer person and a career educator. I started as a paraprofessional in a classroom for autistic students in Saint Paul Public Schools. I continued my career as a cross-categorical special education teacher in Chicago Public Schools. Educational positions I've held include special education coordinator, dean of students, and assistant administrator in multiple schools and districts in Minnesota and Illinois. In 2015, I served as faculty in the teacher licensure program in emotional and behavioral disorders at the University of Minnesota–Twin Cities. I have advanced degrees in psychology, education, and special education.

In 2016, after our family left Nova, I founded Gender Inclusive Schools, an organization that provides parent and educator training to proactively create safe learning environments for LGBTQ+ young people and to repair school climates following incidents of bias and discrimination. As of 2024, Gender Inclusive Schools has conducted hundreds of in-person professional development sessions in more than one hundred school communities. Our long-term partnerships with school districts, independent schools, and community and for-profit organizations, as well as our contracts to facilitate the Human Rights Campaign Foundation's industry-leading Welcoming Schools professional development modules, have allowed us to participate in the education of thousands of individuals across the United States, Canada, Australia, and the United Kingdom.

I am a proud husband to my wife, Hannah, and together we delight in our two beautiful children, Hildie and Dahlia. Hannah is the director of Transforming Families Minnesota, our state's largest and longest-running support network for families with gender-expansive young people. Hildie, our older daughter, advocates for young people like her through performing, acting, and speaking opportunities across the country. In 2022, at age eleven, she was the youngest grand marshal in Twin Cities Pride Parade history. She has appeared in commercials for Expedia and the Human Rights Campaign and has participated in large-scale events with the United States Department of Education. Our younger daughter, Dahlia, is a fierce advocate and ally who amazes everyone around her with her kindness and strength.

Creating safe schools for LGBTQ+ students is a joyful pursuit for our family. The common motivating factor across our family's advocacy work is celebrating gender-expansive children and preventing unnecessary harm to them. I'm so glad you've decided to join us in this work!

About This Book

Thank you for finding this book and beginning—or continuing—your journey to create gender-inclusive schools. If you currently work in or interact with school settings, you know firsthand how critical safe spaces are for LGBTQ+ students. I'm sure you know that inclusion work can be challenging, uncomfortable, and sometimes isolating. But striving to make safe spaces a reality can also be joyful! Know that you have a home in the Gender Inclusive Schools community and that people all around the world, like you, are ready to do the necessary work to create the schools our students deserve.

This book provides practical guidance and resources to help you proactively create educational environments that celebrate, respect, and protect gender-expansive students as their full and authentic selves. It is my sincere hope that this book supports you and other people in school communities to move beyond managing crises, both real and manufactured, so you can attend to the central question: *What do gender-expansive students need from their school communities to thrive?*

Who This Book Is For

This book focuses on practical resources for educators, but it is relevant to all members of school communities. Classroom teachers, front office staff, administrators, social workers, school counselors, teaching assistants, building engineers, psychologists, school board members, and families will all find useful information, reflection opportunities, and activities here. This book is for parents and guardians who are learning about queer identities and families who are wondering what school supports to seek for their queer children. All school community members need to be able to create and contribute to spaces that allow gender-expansive students to participate fully in all school opportunities. School climates are safest when they are predictably safe.

School Climates for Gender-Expansive Students

The educational landscape for gender-expansive students has changed significantly since 2016, when I started doing this work. At that time, many schools were uncertain how to support their first openly transgender students. By now these same school communities have likely navigated support for multiple gender-expansive students in prekindergarten through twelfth grade. No matter where in the United States or Canada a school is located, openly trans students are likely present there.

Best practices for supporting gender-expansive students are no longer hypothetical. And the disasters some predicted if transgender students were treated equitably have failed to materialize. For example, access to facilities for trans youth has not resulted in an epidemic of cisgender boys claiming to be transgender in order to enter "girls'" spaces. Trans inclusion on athletic teams has not led to the dismantling of women's sports. No evidence has emerged to show that affirming gender-expansive kids leads to widespread gender confusion in the general population. The states of California and New York, and large school districts in the cities of Chicago and Washington, DC, have affirming policies for transgender students that have changed very little since their implementation almost a decade ago. Thousands of schools, serving hundreds of thousands of students, have spent years reflecting on and fine-tuning affirming climates for gender-expansive students.

Decision-makers in school communities do not need to reinvent the wheel to support gender-expansive students because the work has already been done. The recommendations in this book are the result of the efforts of countless students, educators, parents, community members, and advocates—and the researchers who have documented the impact of these efforts. This book is informed by trainings I've led in hundreds of independent and public schools across urban and rural communities, the consultations I've provided to families during crises of bullying and discrimination, and the lived experience of my own family.

Gender-expansive kids are everywhere. And they deserve to be safe everywhere they go.

Using This Book

You can engage with this book in a variety of ways. The content is organized to provide quick answers and resources for common concerns that school staff and administrators encounter. For example, if you are struggling with a student's pronouns, head right to chapter 7, Names and Pronouns, for scripts and practice sheets. If you're engaged in whole-staff development, your group can use this book as a road map to work toward equitable systems and practices for gender-expansive students. If your school community has recently passed a gender-inclusion policy or other broad guidance on supporting gender-expansive students, you can use this book to explore and assess its day-to-day implementation. Finally, you can use this book as a checklist of high-impact strategies every educator should have in their tool belt.

What's Included

Chapters 1 and 2 introduce the guiding principles of a gender-inclusive school climate and the vital skill of responding to challenging questions and comments. Chapters 3 through 10 discuss eight important aspects of school life for gender-expansive students. Each of these chapters ends with the following three common features:

- **Guiding Principles Check-In:** This check-in helps you reflect on the guiding principles of supporting happy, healthy kids and protecting privacy and confidentiality.

- **Responding to Challenging Questions and Comments:** This feature offers several chapter-specific role-play prompts that model scenarios you are likely to encounter in your school community. For example, how do you respond to a parent saying, "I don't want a boy in the restroom with my daughter"? These comments or questions come directly from the real world. You may find them shocking or all-too-ordinary, depending on your experiences. The suggested responses can help you check your understanding and prepare for challenging scenarios before they play out in real time.

- **Review and Reflection:** Each chapter concludes with a quick summary of the content followed by an opportunity to reflect on or expand your personal journey toward creating gender-inclusive schools. It might be an activity to increase your empathy for the experiences of gender-expansive students, a chance to evaluate your learning community, or space to plan action steps for making concrete changes in the classroom. If you are reading this book with a professional learning community (PLC), you can use the Review and Reflection section for collaboration and discussion with your group.

The Words of Hope and Optimism concluding chapter reminds you that your everyday efforts matter and encourages you to keep going. This final chapter is followed by a list of valuable resources from national LGBTQ+ organizations, such as lesson plans, recommended books and other media, and structured tools for building safe and affirming school climates.

What's Not Included

This book provides key information, high-impact strategies, and hands-on tools that can help schools on their journeys toward becoming affirming spaces for gender-expansive students. It is not a comprehensive textbook or handbook that addresses every important aspect of creating such spaces. For example, it does not explore ways to create queer-inclusive curriculum across academic content. Nor does it discuss how to form or run a Genders and Sexualities Alliance (GSA), a student-led organization that brings queer and allied youth together to build community and advocate on issues that affect them. This book also does not address any content outside of school settings. Many wonderful texts provide a more comprehensive history of gender identity, LGBTQ+ history, parenting LGBTQ+ children, gender-affirming healthcare, and legal guidelines. Please see the Recommended Resources section at the end of the book for links to advocates and experts on a variety of related important topics.

Terms and Definitions

Whether you are reading this text with a vast LGBTQ+ vocabulary or have little background knowledge on LGBTQ+ topics, it's helpful to begin with shared understanding. This is especially important if you are using this book with a PLC or other study group. Using common language promotes accurate and productive discussion. The following definitions offer a starting point for those discussions. Be aware that language is constantly evolving, so these definitions will likely change over time to reflect the language queer people use to describe their own community.

The following terms come from the Model Gender-Inclusion Policy of Gender Inclusive Schools (see page 105).

Gender identity: One's innermost concept of self as male, female, a blend of both, or neither; how individuals perceive themselves and what they call themselves. One's gender identity can be the same as or different from one's sex assigned at birth.

Transgender: Having a gender identity and/or expression different from cultural expectations based on one's sex assigned at birth. The prefix *trans* means "on the other side of."

Cisgender: Having a gender identity that aligns with one's sex assigned at birth. The prefix *cis* means "on the same side of."

Gender binary: The conceptual classification of gender into two distinct forms—male and female—whether by social system, cultural belief, or both simultaneously.

Nonbinary: Not identifying exclusively as a man or a woman. A nonbinary person may identify as both a man and a woman, somewhere in between, or completely outside these categories. Many—but not all—nonbinary people also identify as transgender.

Gender expansive: Having a gender expression, gender identity, and lived experiences that transcend societal expectations for one's sex assigned at birth; often used in research literature to describe people who are not cisgender.

Intersex: An umbrella term for unique variations in reproductive or sex anatomy. Variations may appear in a person's chromosomes, genitals, or internal organs like testes or ovaries. Some intersex traits are identified at birth, while others may not be discovered until puberty or later in life (Interact 2021).

Gender-affirming care: Developmentally appropriate care oriented toward understanding and appreciating a person's gender experience. This care consists of an array of services that may include medical, mental health, surgical, and nonmedical services for transgender and nonbinary people (Rafferty et al. 2018). For gender-expansive children, early access to gender-affirming care allows them to focus on their social transition and is crucial to overall health and well-being.

Gender dysphoria: Distress arising from conflict between gender identity and sex assigned at birth.

Gender expression: A person's gender-related appearance and behavior, whether or not stereotypically associated with their assigned sex at birth. People who adopt a presentation that varies from stereotypical gender expectations may describe themselves as gender nonconforming, genderqueer, or gender-fluid.

Gender transition: The process by which some people strive to more closely align their internal knowledge of their gender with their outward expression.

LGBTQ+: Lesbian, gay, bisexual, transgender, queer, plus other identities and orientations. *Plus* refers to the many other terms used by people to describe their gender identity and sexual orientation.

Queer: Having a gender expression, gender identity, or sexual orientation that is not straight and/or cisgender. Sometimes used interchangeably with LGBTQ+. The word *queer* has a derogatory history and associations with violence against LGBTQ+ people. Many LGBTQ+ people have reclaimed this term, but some individuals do not use it to describe who they are because of negative lived experiences and trauma. *Queer* is increasingly being used as a standardized term in educational research.

Sexual orientation: A person's emotional, romantic, sexual attraction to another person based on the gender of the other person. Common terms used to describe sexual orientation include but are not limited to *heterosexual*, *asexual*, *lesbian*, *gay*, and *bisexual*. Sexual orientation and gender identity are different.

SOGIE: Acronym that stands for *sexual orientation and gender identity or expression*, pronounced SO-jee.

If you're engaging in new learning on LGBTQ+ topics, much of the content in this book—and even the definitions in this introduction—may lead you to feel overwhelmed or anxious. It's okay to feel that way. Be patient with yourself. Keep your focus on progress, not perfection. Everyone reading this book is starting with a unique set of life experiences and background knowledge. No one expects you to become an immediate expert on every aspect of supporting gender-expansive students.

One of the messages I emphasize in my professional development sessions is this: "You don't have to fully understand someone's identity to not harm them." No matter where you are in your thinking and learning, you can always be respectful and kind. For example, if you don't fully understand or are having trouble conceptualizing nonbinary pronouns, this needn't stop you from using *they/them* anyway. Practice informs understanding just as much as understanding informs practice.

Supporting gender-expansive students in your school community, particularly at a time of peak misinformation and hostility directed at LGBTQ+ people, is a meaningful way to make the world a better place. Everyone reading this book can make a positive impact on children's lives.

Gathering Information

School communities are at different points in their journeys toward supporting and celebrating gender-expansive students. It is powerful to gather relevant information about the current state of gender-inclusive practices in your learning environment before setting goals for the future. It's also important to gauge the the resources and supports available to your staff.

The following Gender-Inclusive Practices Assessment form provides an opportunity to check on the implementation of actions that lead to safer schools for gender-expansive students. I offer this assessment tool to schools ahead of my workshops because it's extremely helpful to have hard data to inform the focus of our time together. Collaborative conversations with school leadership can begin with, "I noticed this pattern in the responses from staff, and here are some options for working toward a solution during our time together." All educators' voices can then be considered instead of only the loudest ones.

Assessment items focus on visible expression of the principles and practices described in this book. This form also highlights fidelity or discrepancies between the intention of policies and the day-to-day implementation of values expressed in those policies.

Gender-Inclusive Practices Assessment

This assessment tool can help you and your school community get an accurate picture of your progress toward gender inclusion. Rank each indicator based on your experiences. If you don't understand an item, or if you don't have personal knowledge of the practices described, select "unsure." If the item does not apply to your school community, select "not applicable."

Key:

1 = strongly agree	4 = disagree	NA = not applicable
2 = agree	5 = strongly disagree	
3 = neither agree nor disagree	U = unsure	

School Policies and Facilities Access	1	2	3	4	5	U	NA
School board policies describing inclusive practices for gender-expansive students/staff/families exist and are easily accessible to the community.							
School antidiscrimination and antibullying statements enumerate protections for gender identity, sexual orientation, and gender expression.							
School has clearly communicated procedures for reporting and repairing bullying behavior when it occurs.							
LGBTQ+ people are visibly present in school marketing materials and on school websites.							
Student dress policies are gender neutral.							
All students have convenient access to restrooms with enhanced privacy during transitions between classes and activities.							
All students have convenient access to enhanced privacy options for changing clothes in locker rooms.							
Familes are proactively informed of the district's policies on supporting LGBTQ+ students, and policy documents are easily accessible online.							
Students can participate in the sports and activities that match their gender identity.							
Student privacy policies state clearly that all information related to a student's LGBTQ+ status is confidential.							

→

Training and Development on LGBTQ+ Topics	1	2	3	4	5	U	NA
School staff have received professional development on inclusion of gender-expansive students.							
Families have been offered training on inclusion of and school-based supports for gender-expansive students.							
Training for school staff on LGBTQ+ topics is provided at regular intervals to ensure new staff have access to best practices.							
Students are provided age-appropriate instruction on commonly used LGBTQ+ terms to describe the identities of their classmates, school staff members, and the parents and caregivers of their peers.							
Student LGBTQ+ affinity groups, such as gender and sexuality alliances (GSAs), receive faculty guidance and support consistent with other clubs and campus organizations.							

Inclusive Language and Honoring Names and Pronouns	1	2	3	4	5	U	NA
School written communication includes children and families of diverse genders and family structures and does not rely on binary gender stereotypes.							
Student information systems provide an opportunity for students to update their names/gender markers if different from their birth certificates.							
School communicates to all stakeholders the importance of using the names and pronouns community members ask them to use.							
Students receive informal and confidential opportunities to share their names/pronouns at regular intervals over the course of the school year.							

Inclusive Classroom Practices	1	2	3	4	5	U	NA
School staff use instructional groupings that do not separate students by gender.							
School staff use gender-neutral language to address large groups of students.							
LGBTQ+ people are represented in curricula and lesson plans multiple times over the school year.							
Students have access to LGBTQ+ books and media in the school library.							
Students have participated in a classroom activity or assignment this school year that examines gender expression, gender identity, or gender stereotypes.							
Social-emotional curriculum includes a focus on the many aspects of identity students hold.							
There are visible displays of support for LGBTQ+ people (such as posters, flags, and other displays) on school walls and in physical spaces.							

→

Personal Perceptions of Gender Inclusivity	1	2	3	4	5	U	NA
Our school is a safe place for gender-expansive people to be their authentic selves.							
Our school affirms and celebrates the existence of LGBTQ+ community members.							
I feel prepared to support a student who changes their name/pronouns in my classroom.							
I feel that my students have the background knowledge necessary to be kind and respectful of gender-expansive people in our school community.							
I feel supported by school leadership in pursuing gender-inclusive practices with my students.							
Instruction on LGBTQ+ topics is consistent across all staff members and classrooms at our school.							
I am comfortable explaining and justifying our school's gender-inclusive practices to my students and their families.							
I have access to and am comfortable providing resources to share with parents/caregivers on LGBTQ+ topics.							
All school staff interrupt and address gender-based bias and discrimination when they observe it at school.							
I feel supported by school leadership when I interrupt and address gender-based bias and discrimination at school.							
I regularly interact with LGBTQ+ people in my life outside our school community.							
It is safe for my LGBTQ+ colleagues to share their identities with colleagues, students, and families.							
Outside factors in our community do not prevent staff from doing what's best for our students at school.							

CHAPTER 1

Guiding Principles

What are the values of your school community? Take a minute to locate the mission or vision statement of your school or district. What does it say? In what ways does it match or not match the experiences of the students and staff in your building? Use the Mission/Vison Reflection form at the end of this chapter as a guide for your reflection.

Your school or district's mission statement likely focuses on student outcomes. The community's stated goal or purpose may be guiding students "to be college and career ready," "to become lifelong learners and global citizens," or "to make positive contributions to society to the best of their ability." One district near me says that its mission is "to inspire and prepare each and every scholar" with courage, confidence, and competence. It doesn't say "to inspire and prepare *some* students." It says, "to inspire and prepare *each and every scholar*." Whether explicitly or implicitly, school communities usually state that their goals apply to all their students. But how many schools can say confidently that every decision they make is for the good of all students?

A school community can monitor which students it is serving well by breaking down student outcomes data according to student demographics. No data set is perfect, of course. But large disparities among demographic groups in achievement, completion, or attendance can show which students are having an adverse or inequitable educational experience.

If data suggests a school's student outcome goals are possible for one group of students, but another group of students is not achieving these goals, a different course of action is needed for the latter students. A school can first ask, "What do our students need?" Then it can work backward from its mission statement to find the (often complex) answers. It must name the systems and procedures creating inequitable experiences for children, then actively pursue replacement actions proven to help.

For example, let's say a school community wants to better understand its suspensions and expulsions. Staff can dive into the data on office discipline referrals (ODRs). They can ask, "Does the frequency of ODRs differ from one population to another?

What are the most common reasons listed for the ODRs?" They might find that students of color are receiving ODRs for insubordination at disproportionately high rates and decide that they can prevent some ODRs by working harder to build culturally responsive relationships before conflict occurs. By using a lens of evaluation and adaptation, this community is focusing on student outcomes and the adult actions that can lead to desired outcomes. It is proactively creating a safer, more effective learning environment.

The rest of this chapter describes two guiding principles that proactively create safe learning environments for gender-expansive students by addressing inequities head-on. They are: (1) *support happy and healthy kids* and (2) *protect privacy and confidentiality*. Each principle is reflected in every piece of guidance in this book. At the ends of chapters 3 through 10, you'll find additional chapter-related discussion of these principles in the Guiding Principles Check-Ins.

Guiding Principle 1: Support Happy and Healthy Kids

Ensuring that students are happy and healthy at school encourages optimum development and prepares them to lead fulfilling and productive lives after they leave school. Using this principle means evaluating choices based on whether they support *all* students' happiness and health. To evaluate choices, ask yourself these two questions: Do your school's policies promote the comfort of adults or the safety and well-being of students? Are your decisions laser-focused on student needs, or are outside factors or politics getting in the way of pursuing best education practices?

Exceptionalities and Experts

When children have exceptional characteristics, in most cases their parents trust doctors, mental health professionals, or other experts to give them sound advice to foster their children's happiness and health. For example, if your child has an IQ of 160, you turn to professional educators and physicians who have experience working with highly gifted children for help determining the accommodations and supports your child needs. If your child has an uncommon medical condition, you seek out experts in that specific field.

As parents of children with multiple exceptional characteristics, Hannah and I often collaborate with our health-care and educational teams. We ask questions. We read books and educate ourselves, and sometimes we push back when we disagree with the team's recommendations. Even then, we respect their expertise and work out a plan together. We understand that our knowledge on a variety of education and gender topics is no substitute for the decades of training and on-the-job experience upon which the experts in our lives draw to make their recommendations.

Among the medical, psychological, and educational professional organizations responsible for promoting the health and well-being of children, there is no debate about what gender-expansive young people need to be happy and healthy. Best practice is gender-affirming care—developmentally appropriate care oriented toward understanding and appreciating a child's gender experience. Following is a list of the youth-serving organizations of experts who endorse the gender-affirming care model as best practice for supporting happy and healthy kids:

- American Academy of Child and Adolescent Psychiatry
- American Academy of Pediatrics
- American Psychiatric Association
- American Psychological Association
- National Association of Elementary School Principals
- National Association of Independent Schools
- National Association of Secondary School Principals
- National Association of School Nurses
- National Association of School Psychologists
- National Association of School Social Workers
- National Education Association
- National PTA
- National School Boards Association
- School Social Work Association of America

As you look through the list, you'll probably notice that the members of these professions have historically been respected individuals in our society. These are the people to whom most families turn when they are at their most vulnerable, when their child's circumstances require reaching beyond their personal knowledge. When these organizations issue position statements, their guidance is derived from providing care to tens of thousands of children every single day.

Though research continues to evolve and inform recommendations for educators in school settings, the evidence supporting a gender-affirming, inclusive, accepting approach is strong. Following are a few highlights from this evidence:

- Longitudinal, large-sample studies demonstrate that transgender children who are affirmed in their identities have mental health that is no different than the mental health of their cisgender peers (Olson et al. 2016).

- Affirming and respecting gender-expansive young people's identities leads to better mental health.

  › Gender-expansive young people who reported acceptance from at least one adult had one-third lower odds of reporting a past-year suicide attempt (Price and Green 2023).

> Acceptance from at least one peer also lowered the odds of a past-year suicide attempt (Price and Green 2023).

> Positive outcomes increase exponentially with each additional setting using a student's affirmed name and pronouns (Russell et al. 2018).

● So-called detransitioning (stopping and/or reversing health care related to a person's social or medical transition) has been greatly exaggerated and misrepresented to justify bans on gender-affirming care and other anti-trans legislation. Recent findings show that less than 1 percent of transgender people receiving gender-affirming care report regret or dissatisfaction with their decisions (Bustos et al. 2021; Olson et al. 2022).

Ask yourself: Are we following the recommendations of experts? Are we letting people who don't have our gender-expansive students' best interests at heart shape the daily supports we provide? Are we somewhere in between?

Supporting Happy and Healthy Kids, or Legally Required to Not Discriminate?

To think a little more deeply about equity and the rights of students in public schools, consider the case of Diane Cowan of Cleveland, Mississippi. A railroad track runs through the middle of Cleveland, dividing its White and Black communities. White residents live on the west side of the tracks; Black residents on the east side. In the early 1960s, Cleveland's schools were officially segregated by race. Segregated schools had been declared unconstitutional in the 1954 US Supreme Court decision *Brown v. Board of Education*, but Cleveland's schools had failed to integrate. When Cowan was a fourth grader at an all-Black elementary school in Cleveland in 1965, she became the first named plantiff in a federal lawsuit to desegregate her school district. The judge ruled in Cowan's favor that Cleveland schools must desegregate. However, the district resorted to alternative tactics to maintain the status quo—establishing "dual residency" policies that made it easier to cheat, assigning teachers to schools based on race, and building new all-Black schools. Legal challenges continued into the early 2000s. In 2011, despite repeated legal rulings and orders to comply, the student population at Cleveland's East High School remained 99.7 percent Black in a district where Black students made up only 67 percent of the total student population. A judge ruled in 2016 that Cleveland had to combine its high schools and end segregation. Cowan was fifty-seven by then (Domonoske 2016).

The Cleveland, Mississippi, case is not unusual. In many locations across the United States, desegregation cases remain open. As recently as 2022, the US Department of Justice had nearly 140 open desegregation cases on its docket, and nearly 18.5 million US students attended segregated schools (Clarke 2023).

The struggle for queer liberation in US educational settings is not equivalent to the fight for racial justice in schools, but the latter demonstrates that educational best practice cannot rely solely on legal guidelines. People don't need a judge to tell them that placing students involuntarily in segregated schools is discriminatory and wrong. Likewise, people don't need legislation to tell them that limiting opportunities for students based on their identities is discriminatory and wrong. There's no need to wait for a law, ruling, or unifying event to begin doing the work necessary for gender-expansive students to thrive in school.

This book is not an argument, so it doesn't refer to individual politicians or mention specific legislation. Nor does this book offer legal guidance. Everyone loses when school communities provide accommodations to gender-expansive kids solely to meet legal requirements. When children are afforded basic decency begrudgingly, *only because it's the law*, they get the message that they aren't inherently worthy of decency. Whatever the circumstances, schools must focus on what they need to do to meet their students' social, emotional, and academic needs at school—to support happy and healthy kids.

Guiding Principle 2: Protect Privacy and Confidentiality

Although this section is shorter, protecting privacy and confidentiality is just as important as supporting happy and healthy kids. Protecting privacy and confidentiality means giving gender-expansive students the right to control all information-sharing related to their identities in school communities. All information related to a student's gender identity and sexual orientation is private data that cannot be shared without consent, just as a student's home address is. The Family Educational Rights and Privacy Act (FERPA) provides clear legal requirements for sharing student data in public schools. However, protecting privacy and confidentiality goes beyond following legal requirements. It is best practice for student safety. Students must be able to control the timing and manner of information sharing about their identities. Safely sharing who they are enables them to be happy and healthy.

Educators should not share any information about a student's identity without the consent of their parents or guardians (and, ideally, also the consent of the student). Before you share student information with colleagues, before you ask students to complete a form or sign up for an activity, before students go on an overnight field trip or walk in a graduation ceremony, ask yourself whether you have honored every student's right to control their information. What this looks like in practice varies greatly depending on students' ages and circumstances. Later chapters offer more specifics, as well as help navigating common conflicts related to social transitions, names and pronouns, and responding to challenging questions and comments.

Review and Reflection

In this chapter, you learned about the two guiding principles that inform the rest of this book. Those principles are:

1. Support happy and healthy kids.
2. Protect privacy and confidentiality.

Use the Guiding Principles Reflection form to reflect on the history of decision-making in your school community and think about how your community could move forward with the guiding principles in mind. Note the positive things your school community is already doing as well as areas for growth. This exercise may help you decide which of the following chapters you want to read next.

Mission/Vision Reflection

Find your school community's mission or vision statement and respond to the following questions and prompts.

Where did you find the mission or vision statement?

Write the full mission statement here.

Which words or phrases stand out to you? Why?

What are some ways in which the educators in your school community are fulfilling the community's expressed values? What are some ways in which educators could do better?

Guiding Principles Reflection

In the space below, describe choices your school community has made that affect gender-expansive students. Do you think these decisions were made to comply with legal requirements or to support happy and healthy kids?

Using the following chart, reflect on positives and areas for growth in your school community related to the guiding principles of supporting happy and healthy kids and protecting privacy and confidentiality. If your school has openly gender-expansive students, how did you learn about their identities? How were decisions made about their access to facilities? How did educators interact with them after they revealed their authentic selves? If you aren't aware of an openly gender-expansive student in your school, consider what would happen if a new gender-expansive student enrolled and showed up at your school tomorrow.

Support Happy and Healthy Kids		Protect Privacy and Confidentiality	
Positives	Areas for Growth	Positives	Areas for Growth

CHAPTER 2

Responding to Challenging Questions and Comments

I t's likely that you hold gender-inclusive beliefs. After all, you're reading this book. It's also likely that you've heard or been part of conversations with challenging questions and comments about gender-inclusive learning communities. How do you respond to biased speech and behaviors in your school community? Do your actions reflect your values?

Educators must respond confidently to defend student safety when comments and behaviors threaten it. This chapter explains why standardized responses are the best strategy and helps you plan and practice standardized responses for a variety of circumstances. As you move through the book, you will read content-specific scenarios and challenging questions or comments with suggested responses in each chapter.

Acknowledging Controversy

Resistance to inclusive practices for LGBTQ+ students is growing across the country. Misinformation is widespread, school board meetings are often full of hate speech, and it seems that every day brings a new law formalizing discrimination against LGBTQ people and their families. As an equity consultant and professional development facilitator, I've had my presentations recorded and posted on social media to whip up hysteria around "what is really going on in our schools." Teachers and administrators in my sessions have gone to news organizations afterward and misrepresented my recommendations. For example, one educator wrote a letter to be read anonymously at a school board meeting; it inaccurately quoted gender identity definitions I provided and took many of my recommendations out of context, sharing half-truths and manufactured "gotcha" moments. Such resistance is not spontaneous. National organizations of "parents' rights" groups are providing the game plan, as well as scripts for turning public comment periods into circuses. This chapter provides language helpful for engaging with members of these groups while minimizing their disruption for students.

"Parents' Rights" Groups

Born out of resistance to COVID-19 safety protocols in public schools, so-called "parents' rights" groups have quickly grown in visibility. These groups often direct their members to engage with their school communities by introducing book bans, opposing inclusion of LGBTQ+ people, blowing up images of "controversial" content they find in their school libraries, and parading around school board meetings. Members often speak about what they believe are the dangers of critical race theory or "gender ideology." Members are frequently associated with disruption to learning environments. The links between these supposedly grassroots organizations and national extremist and hate groups are well documented (SPLC, n.d.). Despite the outsize attention these groups receive, their efforts to transform school boards and learning communities have been largely ineffective. Most of their endorsed school board candidates lost in the November 2023 elections (Goldstein 2023). They did, however, accomplish division and conflict in many school systems.

Hysteria over LGBTQ+ people in school communities will continue to be present for the foreseeable future. To keep hysteria at bay, school communities can present a unified front as they respond to situations that threaten and devalue gender-expansive students. My experience in helping school communities across the United States and Canada has taught me that the best way to keep small problems from becoming big ones is to make sure that all school staff have the language to respond to harmful words in the moment.

QUEER VOICES

I hate when teachers act like my identity is a debate topic or something. I love when teachers just shut things down. Calling something "gay" or making a joke about pronouns is awful. When it comes to hate speech, I just want teachers to make sure it doesn't happen again.

—Sophia, grade nine

Responding in the Moment

Even when staff share a school community's inclusive values, many educators find it difficult to respond productively when they're confronted unexpectedly. Every teacher is human. Humans get nervous.

Imagine a parent or caregiver calling your classroom phone while students are packing up at the end of the day and asking if there will be transgender students in their daughter's cabin on the fifth-grade trip to camp. What would you say? What if they are angry and don't like your response? Maybe you, like most educators, have been conditioned (or actively trained) to avoid conflict between adults in school settings. Given the polarized political climates in the United States and Canada, it's understandable if you feel hesitant to engage with controversial topics.

Educators weigh many variables when responding to any situation. So many factors swirl in their heads during a stressful encounter. For example: Do they have tenure in their school district? Are they brand new to the school? Have they been a leader for more than a decade? Are they responding to show support for an identity they don't hold? Are they feeling on edge because they share identities with a targeted person? Will their administration have their back when they hold expectations?

In 2024, laws prohibiting discussion of sexual orientation and gender identity in schools were present across the United States and Canada. Many of these laws are vaguely worded. While a law can prevent curricular instruction on sexual orientation or gender identity at a particular grade level, school communities still have a responsibility to keep their students and staff safe. It's always okay to create a safe space for every student and every family in your school and classroom.

Practice Builds Confidence

After a confrontation, how many times have you wished you'd said or done something different? It happens to everyone. The rest of this chapter provides opportunities to practice standardized responses so that you will say exactly what you mean—and mean everything you say—in the moment. Practice builds confidence!

The Value of Standardized Responses

When school communities standardize responses to biased statements, it takes the pressure off individuals. When students know that every staff member will respond supportively in the same way, using similar language, every time they hear anti-LGBTQ+ comments or biased speech, students will hopefully feel safe. Standardized responses help students predict how adults will act. This predictability equals safety. By contrast, if students are uncertain whether their identities will be respected or will draw insults and discrimination, they are more likely to feel anxious and unsafe. Standardized staff responses can also provide a powerful model for responsible citizenship and college and career readiness. Responding to discrimination is an important leadership skill for students during and after their K–12 education.

During professional development sessions, I often ask educators to respond to tough questions in the moment to illustrate differences in baseline knowledge. For example, I might pair up participants to role-play a student-teacher scenario. One educator plays the student, and the other plays the teacher. The "student" says, "Alex can't have a pink paper. He's a boy." The "teacher" must provide the first two or three sentences they would use to respond to the comment.

Participants often make inadvertent small mistakes that they can quickly adjust. Someone might say, "I don't know . . . why don't you ask Alex why he likes pink?" This type of response puts unnecessary focus and pressure on Alex to defend himself to an audience. Another person might say something along the lines of, "Boys and girls can like whatever they like." While the intention of this message is positive, it misses a crucial opportunity to acknowledge nonbinary students. A best-practice response would be, "Here at our school, students of all genders can like whatever colors they want. We don't make negative comments about anyone's color choices, so everyone can feel safe." Each subsequent chapter of this book offers content-specific best-practice responses. The following phrases and sentences provide baseline language woven throughout all the recommended responses.

It is important to practice with hypothetical situations before you use these responses in the real world (whenever possible). The experience of responding in the moment, then reflecting and adjusting a response, unlocks the power of preparation and collaboration in developing answers that will have the strongest impact.

Phrases and Sentences with Multiple Applications

"Here at our school . . . "

Example: "Here at our school, kids of all genders can use any of the clothes and props in the dramatic play area."

School communities are cocreated with school staff, district leadership, school boards, students, parents and caregivers, and community members. When your community has decided LGBTQ+ inclusion is part of your core values, you can use these principles as the starting point for expectations. Starting a response with "Here at our school . . . " separates your environment from what is happening in the outside world. It brings focus back to the behavioral expectations for all community members within the school walls and at school functions.

"Public schools are for everyone."

"In places of public accommodation . . . "

Example: "In places of public accommodation, teachers may stop someone from expressing an opinion that interferes with students' learning."

Federal law protects students from discrimination in public schools based on sex (including gender identity, sexual orientation, sex stereotypes, sex characteristics, and pregnancy), race, national origin, age, and disability (OCR 2021; US Department of Education 2024). Furthermore, speech can be limited at school if it substantially disrupts the ability of another child to access their public education (*Tinker v. Des Moines Independent Community School District* 1969). In other words, no one gets to use language in schools that interferes with anyone else's opportunity to learn. By emphasizing this during discussions, you move the conversation away from individual perceptions and beliefs and toward educational access for all students. For independent schools not receiving state or federal funding, these sentence starters can be modified to appeal to the values or established policies school governance has put forth.

"It's not controversial to talk about identities shared by our school community members."

Example: "Sometimes we talk with our second graders about families with two moms or nonbinary parents because it's never controversial to talk about identities shared by our school community members."

If people exist, it's okay to talk about who they are (in broad terms, not gossiping about specific people). The second you shy away from talking about a historically marginalized or excluded group, or act as if the topic is off-limits, you create a second-class member of your school community. LGBTQ+ people exist across the lifespan. You can talk about human diversity across all ages and grade levels.

"Everyone has the right to believe what they believe wherever they are, but the expectations for behavior at home and school are different. Here at school, all students have a right to be safe."

Example: "I understand that you are teaching your child your own values and beliefs about gender. Your child is welcome to believe what they believe, but their actions must meet the expectations we have for all students—including showing respect toward our gender-expansive community members."

Avoid messaging that may be perceived as an attempt to control someone's thoughts or change their privately held beliefs. Educators couldn't do these things even if they wanted to, and everyone has the right to believe whatever they want and teach their children in whatever manner they please. However, the expression of privately held beliefs and their justifications are sometimes incompatible with safe learning environments. If you keep your focus on observable actions and behaviors, not beliefs, you can uphold expectations of respect and safety.

"Kids of all genders can . . . "

Example: "Kids of all genders can like whatever colors they like."

Binary thinking and responses harm nonbinary community members by excluding them. A small shift in language gives room to include all your students. Instead of saying "Boys can do ABC too" or "Girls can wear XYZ," start the sentence with "Kids of all genders can . . . " Acknowledging the complexity of gender reminds all community members that all interests, expressions, activities, colors, professions, and so forth are for everyone.

"Student safety is a higher priority in our school community than adult comfort."
"Being uncomfortable isn't the same thing as being unsafe."

Example: "I understand that some of these concepts may be new for you and your family, and you may have some uncomfortable feelings. However, the inclusion practices at our school are designed to protect the safety of all our students. We won't make changes based on your comfort that create an unsafe environment for your child's peers."

New learning often feels uncomfortable. When you learn new information that doesn't match your previous understanding, you might feel confused and apprehensive. It can be unpleasant. This is normal and natural, but discomfort about a topic is not a reason to avoid it. In school communities new to openly discussing and affirming LGBTQ+ identities, people may disengage after making mistakes. It is okay to feel embarrassed or awkward, but these emotions (as long as you don't feel threatened or unsafe) must take a back seat to the safety of children at your school. When you are discussing systems, be mindful of falling back on what is "least disruptive"—which often just means "most comfortable." Are decisions student-focused or adult-focused? All school initiatives must center the needs of students.

"I can't talk to you about a specific student because of our privacy guidelines, but I can talk to you about our school policies."

Example: "I know your child came home talking about one of their classmates today, and you may be curious about this student. However, in order to uphold our privacy guidelines, I don't share specific students' personal information without their consent. Do you have a question about our inclusion policies or practices?"

No school community member (except one whose professional role might require disclosure) has a right to know private information about individual students. Schools are following the guidelines of personal privacy when they don't publicly (or to other parties) discuss a punishment that child receives for behavior or the services a student receives for a special need. All information related to a student's sexual orientation and gender identity is private medical data. School staff may not disclose any information about a gender-expansive student's school experience to the larger community, the same way they wouldn't share any other personally identifiable information.

"Are we talking about a hypothetical situation or an instance where harm has already happened?"

Example: "You've expressed concerns about students going in and out of bathrooms that don't match their gender identity. Did your child have an experience that made them feel unsafe, or is this a hypothetical concern? We have behavior expectations for all students' behavior in the bathroom, and I want to make sure we are talking about the same thing."

School staff spend an extraordinary amount of time having conversations that could be shortened (or avoided) by using this response. It's important to acknowledge fear, but making plans to address hypothetical concerns is usually a waste of crucial time and resources. Are you responding to a question that does not have a practical application? Can you look to schools that have already gone through change related to the inclusion of gender-expansive students and determine that the issue at hand is likely not going to be an issue moving forward? Some people use hypothetical situations to get around the right to privacy. If you are being asked to discuss a "hypothetical" child who resembles an actual student, you can and should invoke the right of all students to privacy.

Guiding Principles Check-In

Support Happy and Healthy Kids: These standardized responses to challenging questions and comments center the happiness and health of students. Safe students are happy and healthy students. When adults take over the burden of responding to biased comments at school, students have more energy and headspace to focus on the reason they are attending school: learning.

Protect Privacy and Confidentiality: To protect privacy and confidentiality, you can't always answer questions from community members. A student's right to control information related to their gender identity and sexual orientation takes priority over the curiosity and comfort of a third party.

Review and Reflection

This chapter establishes standard language members of your school community can use to respond to challenging questions and comments. Rehearse these!

- "Here at our school . . . "
- "Public schools are for everyone."
- "In places of public accommodation . . . "
- "It's not controversial to talk about identities shared by our school community members."
- "Everyone has the right to believe what they believe wherever they are, but the expectations for behavior at home and school are different. Here at school, all students have a right to be safe."
- "Kids of all genders can . . . "
- "Student safety is a higher priority in our school community than adult comfort."
- "Being uncomfortable isn't the same thing as feeling unsafe."
- "I can't talk to you about a specific student because of privacy guidelines, but I can talk to you about our school policies."
- "Are we talking about a hypothetical situation or an instance where harm has already happened?"

Take a moment to review these phrases and sentences and reflect on the following:

- Have you heard any of these responses used at your school?
- Would your expectations implied by the phrase *here at our school* match your colleauges' expectations?
- How can you connect these responses to the community guidelines already in place at your school?

In the upcoming chapters, you will find many responses to situations I have encountered often in my work with schools. When you are looking for answers to challenging questions or comments on gender or LGBTQ+ topics, check the Responses to Challenging Questions and Comments sections first. You can use similar language, and it's likely that adapting one of these responses will be easiest. If you find that you are entering new territory, you can use the Standardizing Responses form as a framework for establishing responses to new questions or circumstances.

Standardizing Responses

What is the challenging question or circumstance that needs to be addressed?

What are your school community's values or safety concerns that need to be centered?

Clearly state the behavioral expectations that need to be communicated.

Write two or three sentences you suggest as standard responses for your school community.

CHAPTER 3

Social Transitions

The term *social transition* refers to the steps someone might take to match their outward appearance and expression of their gender with their inner experience of self. A person may make changes to their hair, their clothing, their name and pronouns, or a variety of other ways they present themself to the world. A social transition does not follow a standard sequence of steps; the process is unique for each person. Because social transition is so individualized, schools should tailor their support to each student's needs. This chapter offers background information on social transitions, helpful strategies for supporting gender-expansive students, and guidelines on how to communicate about gender transitions.

Consider for a moment how you would respond to this email from a family about their child's upcoming social transition.

Good Morning!

After some wonderful conversations this weekend, Alex is ready to have their identity recognized by their classmates at Woodland Elementary. They will be using the name Alex moving forward, and their pronouns are they/them. We would like to sit down with you, as Alex's classroom teacher, and someone from the admin team to clarify specifics on facilities access, names and pronouns, and privacy, and to plan how to inform Alex's classmates about these changes. Alex wants to start going by their new name and pronouns in the next few days. Could we meet Monday morning in person or by video call? It's important that we speak soon so Alex feels supported and affirmed at school. We are so excited for them to be their full self at school! We are keeping our cell phones handy and will be checking email frequently. We're looking forward to working together to get this done quickly!

The Johnson Family

After reading the email from Alex's family, would you feel confident about next steps? Who should you share this information with? How would you respond to Alex's family? Would you have any questions for them? How would you inform Alex's peers? How could you make sure your school follows the principles of supporting happy and healthy kids and protecting privacy and confidentiality?

These questions are all important aspects of helping students, families, caregivers, and school staff navigate social transitions, because they involve information transfer and decision making that may have a significant impact on school actions and student experiences.

A Significant Moment

Social transitions can be low-stakes events or high-stakes events—or both simultaneously—depending on the circumstances. It's developmentally appropriate for children of all ages to explore what being their authentic selves looks like. As part of this exploration, a student may try on a new name or new clothing to see how it fits. After a few days or weeks, they may try on something else—or return to the way they outwardly expressed their gender before. Because such exploration is normal, a child's social transition may be no big deal for them or the people around them. It might also trigger social anxiety or social conflict, especially if they have previously encountered bullying for their gender expression.

Regardless of how it plays out, a social transition is a significant moment. If you're a teacher, your classroom may be the first place a student uses a gender-affirming name that they will use for the rest of their lives. It might be read out loud at the most important milestone events in their education and career. It might be used on their marriage license or their children's birth certificates. It is a privilege to bear witness to this moment and to support your students as they explore their authentic selves.

I encourage you to adopt a mindset that centers the significance of this moment. If possible, channel any feelings of worry and stress into thinking about how you can best support your students. Take this moment as an opportunity to work through action steps in your mind. Remember that communication is key. Communicate with consent. Communicate as much as is needed for all parties to feel confident and to make a student's social transition a happy event that allows them to be their authentic self at school.

If you need support, ask the student or their parent or caregiver for permission to ask questions of a trusted staff member or a district equity liaison. Frame this request as an opportunity for personal growth, not as evidence of a deficit in your abilities as an educator. Model what you want your students to do when they encounter situations that require new learning. For example, after Alex's parents email you about their child's social transition, you might reply, "I'm so excited to support Alex during this important time. Would it be okay if I reach out to a few other district staff members to collaborate on how to respond to questions from other students following a social transition? I have a general idea of how I would respond, but these LGBTQ+ educators might be able to offer their expertise and help me support Alex in the best possible way."

I encourage you to embrace the hope and celebration that social transitions can bring. With a social transition, a gender-expansive student begins a new chapter in their life. The joy of witnessing a child being their authentic self can outweigh any negative emotions.

A Process of Exploration

The journeys of gender-expansive children have as many similarities as differences. Although each child's journey is unique, here are a few things you can keep in mind in all situations:

- **People of all genders can have any number of interests and gender expressions.** A boy wearing a dress isn't necessarily on a journey toward social transition. A child may change their clothing but have no interest in changing their name or pronouns. However, exploration of gender expression helps children understand who they are and may lead to outward changes that reflect who they know themselves to be.

- **Supporting a child who is exploring their gender is not a burden.** Learning to use new pronouns and names can be tricky. If you're feeling frustrated about the learning curve and its impact on your daily teaching practices, try to step back a bit and quantify the impact. For example, when I hear an educator in one of my professional development sessions say something like, "I can't spend my whole day trying to figure out which pronouns a student is using this week," I open a conversation about the actual amount of time they are spending on such accommodations. I ask the educator, "How many students have sought support in changing their name and pronouns this year? Of those students, how many have changed their name and pronouns more than once? For those students, how many minutes have you spent this year updating student records or practicing pronouns?" The actual amount of time the educator spends supporting social transitions is usually negligible compared to that spent on other tasks over the school year. And the small amount of time spent affirming students in their gender is time very well spent because of its positive impacts on the students' mental health. When a student no longer has to hide their identity or chafe at responding to names and pronouns that don't reflect it, they can focus their full attention on learning. When a student is addressed as the correct gender because they have socially transitioned with a new haircut or clothing or name and pronouns, they may feel a strong sense of well-being as people recognize them for their true self.

- **You don't need to weigh in on whether you think a student is serious about their social transition.** Can you imagine the courage it takes for a child to ask an adult outside their family to call them by a different name and use new pronouns? Remember that social transitions aren't permanent. It's okay for a student to experiment until they find what fits them. And it's *not* okay for you pass judgment on them. I have yet to encounter a child who experienced harm because they were allowed to socially transition. The worst-case scenario when you support a child's social transition is that they learn that you care deeply about their happiness and well-being.

Informing a Student's Peers

A student's needs and comfort level should guide the timing and manner of their social transition. School staff should never accelerate, delay, encourage, or discourage a student in sharing information about their gender with classmates. Though these actions may come from supportive or protective intentions, pushing a student before they are ready and acting as if their identity is a problem are equally harmful. For example, school staff may say, "Can you wait a week so that we can get our policies in order?" or, "We have time in morning meeting this morning; why don't we get your announcement out of the way before our next unit starts in a few days?" Student transitions can be urgent, and the decision to share a transition publicly often comes after an already-too-long wait to live authentically. Any time a child spends pretending to be something they aren't raises their risk of harm. Likewise, encouraging a child to share their transition publicly before they are ready can infringe on their agency as a person. If they aren't ready, they aren't ready. Educators should not insert their own conditions or influence on this important moment.

I thought about telling my parents I was trans for a long time. It was probably over a year after I first told my friends that I finally came out to my mom and dad. After I told them, and we started using my name, it felt like such a relief. Using my deadname at school seemed impossible. It wasn't me anymore, and once I stopped pretending at home, pretending at school made my anxiety go through the roof. It felt different, and it just wasn't okay anymore.

—Noah, grade nine

Small moments in students' school experiences can add up to a large cumulative impact. You don't know each child's circumstances in detail. Therefore, you can't predict exactly when a negative experience will cross from something they can deal with into a crisis situation.

There is no single best way for every gender-expansive student to communicate about a social transition. Some students want to communicate through a simple announcement, such as, "This is Alex, and they use they/them pronouns. One of the ways we show respect to our classmates is by using the name and pronouns they ask us to use." Other students will want to share more information or have an open discussion. Make sure that whoever is moderating these discussions is confident and comfortable at redirecting harmful language or behaviors that may occur. A social

When I was in second grade, I wanted my classmates to know that I was a trans girl. My teacher read [us] a book about Jazz Jennings called *I Am Jazz*. When the book was over, the teacher asked each of my friends how they might be the same as or different from Jazz. One student said, "I'm like Jazz because I like to swim." Another student said, "I'm not like Jazz because I don't have any siblings." When it was my turn, I said, "I am like Jazz because I'm a transgender girl." I think a lot of the adults were worried that something bad might happen, because the principal and counselor were in the room. Most of my classmates just shrugged when I told them who I was. We went and played during recess, and it wasn't really a big deal.

—Hildie, grade eight

transition should be a joyful opportunity for a student to fully realize their authentic self, but it can also be the beginning of targeted bias or discrimination. Because this is an important moment, educators need to be honest about their ability to manage it.

Earlier in the chapter you read a sample email from Alex's family letting their school community know that Alex needed to socially transition. If you received that email, how would you respond? A best-practice response follows. But before reading on, take a moment to compose your own answer or discuss with a colleague.

```
Good afternoon, Johnson Family!

I am so excited for Alex and feel honored to be part of this
important moment in their school career at Woodland! We would
be thrilled to meet with you all on Monday morning before
school. I haven't shared Alex's new information with any of
my colleagues yet because I want to center Alex's privacy as
we let their classmates know about their affirmed name and
pronouns. Would it be okay if I spoke with Principal Beth
to see if she would like to join us for the meeting Monday
morning? During our collaboration, we can talk through some
messaging options and what information Alex would like their
classmates to know. We will follow your lead through this
process, so please don't hesitate to communicate Alex's needs
as soon as they come up. Looking forward to our meeting on
Monday!

Ms. Rosemary
```

Guiding Principles Check-In

Support Happy and Healthy Kids: For every human, living authentically is a huge part of being both happy and healthy. Having to hide an important piece of your identity takes a big toll on physical and mental health, as well as learning ability. Educators must minimize anything that distracts students from learning.

Protect Privacy and Confidentiality: Information related to any student's social transition should be treated with sensitivity and should honor FERPA and the basics of consent outlined in Chapter 1. Staff members should not share any information about a student's identity without permission from the student or their parents. Keep in mind that if a student feels like everyone is talking about them, that is not helpful for their mental health and well-being. Embrace the complexity that comes along with student social transitions. If you're not sure about something, communicate. Ask for consent before sharing information.

Responding to Challenging Questions and Comments

Challenge: *A student laughs when Alex explains their new name and nonbinary pronouns.*

Response: "I'm going to hit pause really quick to remind us all to be respectful. We don't laugh when someone is sharing something personal about who they are."

Challenge: *"I heard (Alex's former name) in my child's class wants to be called Alex."*

Response: "Sometimes the students in our class share personal information with their peers. I don't discuss or share that information with members of the school community unless I have permission. I would follow the same guidelines if someone were asking about your child."

Challenge: *"Is there a transgender student in my child's class?"*

Response: "All information related to our students' gender identity is protected data. I'm not able to talk about any other student's status, but I'm happy to talk with you about your child's needs."

Challenge: *"My dad said there is no such thing as being transgender, and there aren't any options besides being a boy or girl."*

Response: "Everyone has the right to believe what they believe, but here at school, we respect people of all genders by using the name and pronouns they ask us to use. You are expected to show respect to your classmates by following those guidelines while you are at school."

Review and Reflection

In this chapter, you learned about the concept of social transition and how that process can vary from person to person. Though the outward changes a person may show when socially transitioning (such as new clothes, hair, name, and pronouns) may not be permanent, this transition can be an important, powerful, and joyful part of that person's life. This may be the first time other people see the person they are. Being seen as you truly are is a universal human need.

Take a moment to reflect on the following:

- Recall a time in your life when you felt seen by someone important to you.
- Have you ever had someone make incorrect assumptions about who you or your family are?
- How did it feel to either resolve that incorrect information or live with it on a day-to-day basis?

CHAPTER 4

Medical Transitions

Hildie was only five years old the first time Hannah and I were asked, "Is your daughter going to have the surgery?" People who barely know us regularly ask us questions related to her body parts, her development through puberty, what choices we've made, and why and how we've made them. Our experience is common; gender-expansive children and their families often field inappropriate and invasive questions. You can help your students and their families by redirecting intrusive questions and by developing a basic understanding of gender-affirming care.

Bodies Are Private

Bodies are private. Schools have no role to play in gender-affirming medical care. Staff should not encourage or discourage any decisions regarding students' bodies. Nor should they speculate on or discuss the decisions students make with their care teams and families. Put bluntly: if you're an educator, gender-expansive students' medical decisions are none of your business.

Of course, this doesn't mean that others won't insert themselves. The human rights of gender-expansive people are under attack not only in the United States and Canada, but also around the world. Politicians and pundits regularly use the health care of trans people as a political weapon. As of early 2024, for example, twenty-three US states had banned gender-affirming care for adolescents (Tanne 2024), and similar legislation was unfolding in some Canadian provinces. Such targeting of gender-expansive people may affect the students in your school. Your role, then, is to provide mental health and emotional support for children whose basic human rights are up for debate.

What Is a Medical Transition?

When a person transitions socially, they often change outward markers of their identity, such as their clothing, accessories, hair, makeup, name, pronouns, and/or some behaviors. A medical transition is a collaboration with a health-care team on gender-affirming medical treatments. These treatments may include hormone therapy and/or medical procedures.

Like social transitions, all medical transitions are unique. Gender-expansive people are individuals, so there is no single correct or sequential way to be trans or to transition. Many gender-expansive people transition both socially and medically, but not all do. Any narrative that says all trans people are on a path toward surgery is false. Some people pursue a variety of medically necessary gender-affirming procedures, including surgery. Others do not.

Hearing Directly from an Expert in the Field

While I was writing the rest of this book, I felt very comfortable making school-based recommendations from my personal expertise and experience. But to describe the health-care needs of gender-expansive young people, I knew I needed to collaborate with someone who has spent their career building expertise in this field.

Dr. Kade Goepferd is a medical doctor who has cared for hundreds of gender-expansive kids and collaborated with their families on their essential health care over many years, providing not only routine pediatric care but also supporting patients through moments of celebration and crisis. Goepferd is a leader in the field and is Medical Director of the Gender Health Program and Chief Education Officer at Children's Minnesota. I'm delighted to feature their expert perspective in this chapter to provide educators with the best information available about essential health care for gender-expansive students.

Essential Health Care for Transgender and Gender-Diverse (TGD) Youth: Separating Fact from Fiction

by Kade Goepferd, M.D., Medical Director of the Gender Health Program and Chief Education Officer at Children's Minnesota

The Needs of TGD Youth

As society's understanding and language around gender identity and gender expression have improved, transgender and gender diverse young people have become more visible in communities and schools. Slowly, society has begun to embrace and support the 1 to 3 percent of youth who identify as transgender (Herman, Flores, and O'Neill 2022). But TGD youth still face significant discrimination in their daily lives, including bullying, harassment, and violence (Johns et al. 2019). The discrimination is even worse for transgender youth of color (Trevor Project 2022).

TGD youth also face significant health disparities (Johns et al. 2019). They are chronically medically underserved, as patients and families often don't know where to turn or have to wait several months for care from providers trained to meet their pediatric and adolescent health needs in a way that affirms and supports their gender identities and expressions (Goetz and Arcomano 2023). TGD youth face additional health-care challenges too, such as being misgendered, lacking insurance coverage, or even being refused treatment. They may see providers who ask invasive questions about their personal lives or have limited knowledge about transgender health. They may have to travel long distances to access the health care they need. As of early 2024, legislation restricting access to essential health care for transgender youth had passed in twenty-three states, violating the rights of the youth, their families, and their medical providers.

Because of discrimination and bias, TGD youth are more likely to experience anxiety, depression, and suicidal ideation and attempts (Hisle-Gorman et al. 2021). To improve their physical and mental health outcomes, TGD youth and their families need safe and accepting places to get their questions answered by experts in gender health care. Indeed, TGD youth need specialized health care tailored to their needs, just like any other children with special health-care needs.

The Case for Access to Gender-Affirming Care for TGD Youth

Each child has unique health-care needs. TGD youth have health-care challenges that are different from those of their cisgender peers. When TGD youth have access to essential health care that supports and affirms their identities and expressions, they experience significant improvements in their mental and physical health. Essential health care for transgender youth is supported by decades of research, follows clinical guidelines and protocols, and is a thoughtful, lengthy process that involves partnership between parents, patients, and their clinical care teams. More than two dozen peer-reviewed studies, many published in the last decade in some of the leading medical journals, have demonstrated that:

- Essential health care for TGD youth helps improve patients' sense of self, positive affect, and life satisfaction while decreasing symptoms of anxiety and depression (Chen et al. 2023).

- Transgender and nonbinary youth who were able to access puberty-delaying medications and/or hormone therapy had 60 percent lower odds of depression and 73 percent lower odds of suicidality after just one year (Tordoff et al. 2022).

- Adolescents who received puberty suppression had significantly better psychosocial functioning after twelve months, compared to psychosocial support alone (Costa et al. 2015).

- Despite the fact that TGD youth face discrimination, harassment, and stigmatization, after medical treatment with specialized gender care, they showed similar or better psychological functioning as compared with their cisgender peers (van der Miesen et al. 2020; deVries et al. 2014).

- Timing makes a difference, as accessing essential medical care during adolescence significantly reduced severe psychological distress in adulthood for transgender people (Lee et al. 2023).

The evidence is clear: access to developmentally appropriate, evidence-based, essential health care can be lifesaving for TGD kids. These patients and their families deserve access to health-care professionals who see them, hear them, and believe them.

What We Do in the Gender Health Clinic

First and foremost, gender health clinics provide a supportive environment for children, teens, and families to ask questions of health-care professionals who specialize in the care of TGD youth. Typically, during an initial visit, children and their families meet with a gender health expert to discuss developmental questions or concerns about gender identity and to develop a customized approach to care. Often, youth (especially teenagers) and their families come to this initial consultation with different questions and goals.

Gender health experts can help youth and families understand each other and learn to speak a common language. Questions can range from how to address bullying in school to how parents or caregivers can support their child to what medical interventions may be appropriate. Not every patient who comes to a gender health clinic will need to access all the medical interventions available to them, and many patients will not need any of them. The decision to pursue any medical intervention is a lengthy process. It includes teams of medical providers and mental health professionals who work closely with families to understand their child's experience, needs, and available options. Just like other specialized medical care, health care for TGD youth is supported by evidence-based research and the expert opinion of every major medical society in the United States, including the American Academy of Pediatrics, the American Psychological Association, the Centers for Disease Control and Prevention, and the Society for Adolescent Health and Medicine.

Essential health care for transgender and gender diverse youth is not new or experimental. The first gender clinics in the United States opened at Johns Hopkins Hospital in the 1960s, and the first pediatric gender multispecialty clinic opened at Boston Children's Hospital in 2007. The medications and interventions being used today are largely the same as they were decades ago and follow care guidelines set forth by both the Pediatric Endocrine Society and the World Professional Association for

Transgender Health (Hembree et al. 2017; Coleman et al. 2022). The approach to care for TGD kids aims to understand and support the whole child within the context of their family and community, which includes understanding both their medical and their mental health needs. The child receives a biopsychosocial assessment from a mental health professional as well as appointments with one or more members of a medical health-care team.

For children who have not yet reached puberty, no medical interventions are needed or available. Visits to the gender clinic at these ages focus on providing education to parents about how to approach their child's gender exploration and how to ensure a safe and inclusive environment for their child at home, with extended family members, and at school. Often, providers talk through a social transition or ways that a child may be supported to express their gender identity by letting them choose their clothing, haircut, toy, and playmate options. Sometimes this also means trying a new name or pronoun that better aligns with the child's consistent gender identity and expression. The key is allowing room for exploration and flexibility in a safe and supportive environment.

The onset of puberty can be difficult for many TGD adolescents, and this is the time when medical intervention can begin to make a difference in terms of future health outcomes. While some TGD adolescents are very distressed by their puberty, some are not and don't need to pursue any medical intervention. For patients who experience distress or dysphoria about puberty changes, most gender clinics offer puberty and/or menstrual suppression. Puberty suppression, the pausing of puberty often referred to as "puberty blockers," can be offered to youth once they reach the second stage of puberty (noticeable physical changes). Puberty blockers, which are reversible, are shots or implants that pause puberty for the patient. They have been used for decades to delay the development of gendered puberty changes. For teenagers who have a uterus, medications can prevent menstruation and any associated mental distress or dysphoria. This is often called menstrual suppression, and it is also reversible. It includes medications and treatment options that are commonly used for birth control in adolescents.

For youth who are in middle to late adolescence, gender-affirming hormone treatment with masculinizing or feminizing hormones may be appropriate. These treatments are partially reversible and slowly create puberty changes in the body to align with the patient's gender identity. The decision to move forward with such treatment is typically made with a medical gender health expert, along with a readiness assessment by a mental health professional, as well as the support and consent of parents. Access to hormone therapy can significantly improve the mental health of transgender and gender-diverse adolescents (Chen et al. 2023). Thoughts of suicide and suicide attempt rates significantly decreased for youth who had access to both puberty suppression and gender-affirming hormones (Tordoff et al. 2022). This is why such health care is often referred to as life-saving.

Gender-affirming surgeries are typically not offered to TGD youth; they are most often performed for patients who are eighteen or older. Chest surgeries, such as mastectomies, are rare (less than 0.1 percent of transgender adolescents) and are evaluated on a case-by-case basis. Though this type of surgery is rare, it can be a major source of relief for some older adolescents (Olson-Kennedy et al. 2018), and the regret rates for this type of surgery are incredibly low—less than 1 percent (Bruce et al. 2023; Wiepjes et al. 2018; Narayan et al. 2021; Bustos et al. 2021; Olson-Kennedy et al. 2018). By comparison, knee surgeries have a regret rate of up to 20 percent (Mahdi et al. 2020; Kahlenberg et al. 2018).

How to Support TGD Youth

As health care strives to become more equitable, inclusive, and accessible, TGD kids and families need advocates and allies. These efforts need to extend beyond gender health clinics to all points in their journey, including the significant time they spend in schools.

When children disclose questions about their gender identity, or affirm a gender identity other than what they were assigned at birth, the best initial response from adults in their lives is to support without steering. This allows kids to explore their questions and identities with the knowledge that they can change course as needed. Parents often struggle to know how to best support their kids on top of dealing with their own feelings of grief, anger, disappointment, or fear. School staff can affirm to parents that asking questions is okay and seeking supportive resources is encouraged. Parents often need just as much, if not more, room to ask questions and seek support as they learn more about their child's identity. Parental rejection is a significant risk factor for poor physical and mental health outcomes for transgender youth (Campbell et al. 2023), including a significantly increased risk of suicide, so educators should always encourage parents to consistently reassure their children that they love them, even when they are struggling to understand their expressed identities. Unconditional parental love is the single biggest protective factor to keep TGD kids healthy and safe.

References

Bruce, Lauren, Alexander N. Khouri, Andrew Bolze, Maria Ibarra, Blair Richards, Shokoufeh Khalatbari, Gaines Blasdel, et al. 2023. "Long-Term Regret and Satisfaction with Decision Following Gender-Affirming Mastectomy." *JAMA Surgery* 158 (10): 1070–1077. doi.org/10.1001/jamasurg.2023.3352.

Bustos, Valeria P., Samyd S. Bustos, Andres Mascaro, Gabriel Del Corral, Antonio J. Forte, Pedro Ciudad, Esther A. Kim, Howard N. Langstein, and Oscar J. Manrique. 2021. "Regret after Gender-Affirmation Surgery: A Systematic Review and Meta-Analysis of Prevalence." *Plastic and Reconstructive Surgery Global Open* 9 (3): e3477. doi.org/10.1097/GOX.0000000000003477.

Campbell, Travis, Samuel Mann, Yana van der Meulen Rodgers, and Nathaniel Tran. 2023. "Family Matters: Gender Affirmation and the Mental Health of Transgender Youth." July 6, 2023. *Social Science Research Network*. dx.doi.org/10.2139/ssrn.4503648.

Chen, Diane, Johnny Berona, Yee-Ming Chan, Diane Ehrensaft, Robert Garofalo, Marco A. Hidalgo, Stephen M. Rosenthal, Amy C. Tishelman, and Johanna Olson-Kennedy. 2023. "Psychosocial Functioning in Transgender Youth after 2 Years of Hormones." *New England Journal of Medicine* 388 (3): 240–250. doi.org/10.1056/NEJMoa2206297.

Coleman, E., A. E. Radix, W. P. Bouman, G. R. Brown, A. L. C. deVries, M. B. Deutsch, R. Ettner, et al. 2022. "Standards of Care for the Health of Transgender and Gender Diverse People, Version 8." *International Journal of Transgender Health* 23 (sup1): S1–S259. doi.org/10.1080/26895269.2022.2100644.

Costa, Rosalia, Michael Dunsford, Elin Skagerberg, Victoria Holt, Polly Carmichael, and Marco Colizzi. 2015. "Psychological Support, Puberty Suppression, and Psychosocial Functioning in Adolescents with Gender Dysphoria." *Journal of Sexual Medicine* 12 (11): 2206–2214. doi.org/10.1111/jsm.13034.

deVries, Annelou L. C., Jennifer K. McGuire, Thomas D. Steensma TD, Eva C. F. Wagenaar, Theo A. H. Doreleijers, and Peggy T. Cohen-Kettenis. 2014. "Young Adult Psychological Outcome after Puberty Suppression and Gender Reassignment." *Pediatrics* 134 (4): 696–704. doi.org/10.1542/peds.2013-2958.

Goetz, Teddy G., and Amanda C. Arcomano. 2023. "'Coming Home to My Body': A Qualitative Exploration of Gender-Affirming Care-Seeking and Mental Health." *Journal of Gay and Lesbian Mental Health* 27 (4): 380–400. doi.org/10.1080/19359705.2023.2237841.

Hembree, Wylie C., Peggy C. Cohen-Kettenis, Louis Gooren, Sabine E. Hannema, Walter J. Myer, M. Hassan Murad, Stephen M. Rosenthal, et al. 2017. "Endocrine Treatment of Gender-Dysphoric/Gender-Incongruent Persons: An Society Clinical Practice Guideline." *Journal of Clinical Endocrinology and Metabolism* 102 (11): 3869–3903. doi.org/10.1210/jc.2017-01658.

Herman, Jody L., Andrew R. Flores, and Kathryn K. O'Neill. 2022. *How Many Adults and Youth Identify as Transgender in the United States?* Los Angeles: The Williams Institute, UCLA School of Law. williamsinstitute.law.ucla.edu/wp-content/uploads/Trans-Pop-Update-Jun-2022.pdf.

Hisle-Gorman, Elizabeth, Natash A. Schvey, Terry A. Adirim, Anna K. Rayne, Apryl Susi, Timothy A. Roberts, and David A. Klein. 2021. "Mental Healthcare Utilization of Transgender Youth before and after Affirming Treatment." *Journal of Sexual Medicine* 18 (8): 1444–1454. doi.org/10.1016/j.jsxm.2021.05.014.

Johns, Michelle M., Richard Lowry, Jack Andrzejewski, Lisa C. Barrios, Zewditu Demissie, Timothy McManus, Catherine N. Rasberry, Leah Robin, and J. Michael Underwood. 2019. "Transgender Identity and Experiences of Violence Victimization, Substance Use, Suicide Risk, and Sexual Risk Behaviors among High School Students—19 States and Large Urban School Districts, 2017." *Morbidity and Mortality Weekly Report* 68 (3): 67–71. doi.org/10.15585/mmwr.mm6803a3.

Kahlenberg, Cynthia A., Benedict U. Nwachukwu, Alexander S. McLawhorn, Michael B. Cross, Charles N. Cornell, and Douglas E. Padgett. 2018. "Patient Satisfaction after Total Knee Replacement: A Systematic Review." *HSS Journal* 14 (2): 192–201. doi.org/10.1007/s11420-018-9614-8.

Lee, Min Kyung, Yuehwern Yih, Deanna R. Willis, Janine M. Fogel, and James D. Fortenberry. 2023. "The Impact of Gender-Affirming Medical Care During Adolescence on Adult Health Outcomes among Transgender and Gender Diverse Individuals in the United States: The Role of State-Level Policy Stigma." *LGBT Health* 3 October 2023. doi.org/10.1089/lgbt.2022.0334.

Mahdi, Amir, Mia Svantesson, Per Wretenberg, and Maria Hälleberg-Nyman. 2020. "Patients' Experiences of Discontentment One Year after Total Knee Arthroplasty: A Qualitative Study." *BMC Musculoskeletal Disorders* 21 (1): 29. doi.org/10.1186/s12891-020-3041-y.

Narayan, Sasha Karan, Rayisa Hontscharuk, Sara Danker, Jess Guerriero, Angela Carter, Gaines Blasdel, Rachel Bluebond-Langner, et al. 2021. "Guiding the Conversation: Types of Regret after Gender-Affirming Surgery and Their Associated Etiologies." *Annals of Translational Medicine* 9 (7): 605. doi.org/10.21037/atm-20-6204.

Olson-Kennedy, Johanna, Jonathan Warus, Vivian Okonta, Marvin Belzer, and Lelie F. Clark. 2018. "Chest Reconstruction and Chest Dysphoria in Transmasculine Minors and Young Adults: Comparisons of Nonsurgical and Postsurgical Cohorts." *JAMA Pediatrics* 172 (5): 431–436. doi.org/10.1001/jamapediatrics.2017.5440.

Tordoff, Diana M., Jonathon W. Wanta, Arin Collin, Cesalie Stepney, David J. Inwards-Breland, and Kym Ahrens. 2022. "Mental Health Outcomes in Transgender and Nonbinary Youths Receiving Gender-Affirming Care." *JAMA Network Open* 5 (2): e220978. doi.org/10.1001/jamanetworkopen.2022.0978.

Trevor Project. 2022. *2022 National Survey on LGBTQ Mental Health*. thetrevorproject.org/survey-2022/assets/static/trevor01_2022survey_final.pdf.

van der Miesen, Anna I. R., Thomas D. Steensma, Annelou L. C. de Vries, Henny Bos, and Arne Popma. 2020. "Psychological Functioning in Transgender Adolescents before and after Gender-Affirmative Care Compared with Cisgender General Population Peers." *Journal of Adolescent Health* 66 (6): 699–704. doi.org/10.1016/j.jadohealth.2019.12.018.

Wiepjes, Chantal M., Nienke M. Nota, Christel J. M. de Blok, Maartje Klaver, Annelou L. C. deVries, S. Annelijn Wensing-Kruger, Renate T. de Jongh, et al. 2018. "The Amsterdam Cohort of Gender Dysphoria Study (1972–2015): Trends in Prevalence, Treatment, and Regrets." *Journal of Sexual Medicine* 15 (4): 582–590. doi.org/10.1016/j.jsxm.2018.01.016

Guiding Principles Check-In

Support Happy and Healthy Kids: To support happy and healthy kids, educators must prioritize the practices that are associated with positive outcomes for gender-expansive kids. Gender-affirming care has been shown to increase every measure of student health and well-being. As an educator, you do not have a role in facilitating access to gender-affirming care. However, you must hold other members of your school community accountable when they use speech related to medical transitions that is inappropriate, intrusive, or dehumanizing.

Protect Privacy and Confidentiality: To protect the privacy and confidentiality of students, conversations about any student's body or medical history (or future) must be off-limits. Being gender-expansive does not make one's body more public.

Responding to Challenging Questions and Comments

The following responses to common questions can help you shut down inappropriate conversations. Discussions about what may or may not be happening with the bodies of minor children should be categorically off-limits in school communities. Such discussions reduce gender-expansive people to their bodies and dehumanize and pathologize their existence.

Challenge: *"Children shouldn't be making permanent changes to their bodies."*

Response: "Decisions related to the gender-affirming care of our students are made privately between the students and their families and medical teams. I can't imagine intruding on the private medical decisions of another family."

Response: "We don't entertain discussions about other families' medical choices in our school community and encourage everyone to engage only in conversations that pertain to your own family. If you have broader questions, here are some resources from the major medical and psychological associations that set best-practice care guidelines."

Gender-Affirming Care Resources

> "Gender Identity 5 Years after Social Transition" from *Pediatrics*: publications.aap.org/pediatrics/article/150/2/e2021056082/186992/Gender-Identity-5-Years-After-Social-Transition

> "Gender-Affirming Care of Transgender and Gender-Diverse Youth: Current Concepts" from *Annual Review of Medicine*: annualreviews.org/doi/full/10.1146/annurev-med-043021-032007

> "Urging Congress to Protect Access to Gender-Affirming Care for Transgender Youth" from the American Psychologial Association: apaservices.org/advocacy/news/gender-affirming-care-transgender-youth

Challenge: *"These kids are going through a phase and are confused. I've read studies that say all of these kids end up being gay anyway, so we shouldn't be buying into their delusions when they will regret it later."*

Response: "It's not your job or the job of our staff members to engage in debates about research studies. The expertise of transgender people's lived experience and of their medical and psychological care teams is paramount."

Challenge: *"Why are you encouraging my child to think there is something wrong with their body?"*

Response: "Our school staff have no influence or role to play in encouraging or discouraging medical decisions for our students. We would love to connect you with some community resources that might be helpful if you have questions that are outside our own roles and expertise."

Response: "Is this a hypothetical situation or is there an actual event or circumstance you would like to discuss?"

Challenge: *"Alex has been so moody ever since they started taking hormones."*

Response: "I'm going to remind everyone that speculating about a student's medication is a breach of their right to privacy. Please don't make inferences or connect any student's behavior to medical information they have not given us permission to discuss."

Review and Reflection

This chapter intentionally limits discussion of medical transitions to communicate respect for gender-expansive people's right to privacy and autonomy. It's not the business of educators to insert themselves into the private medical decisions of others. It *is* an educator's business to address disrespectful and intrusive questions and comments about other people's bodies.

As an empathy exercise, hold in your mind a topic about your personal life or family circumstances that you would consider to be off-limits for open discussion at your job. Think of a sensitive topic that you discuss only with family and/or select friends. If a colleague or member of your school community began asking intrusive questions about this topic in a room full of your peers, what might you be thinking or feeling in the moment? What kinds of support would help you navigate this awkward encounter?

CHAPTER 5

Facilities Access

Physical spaces shared in close proximity are often targets for policies that marginalize specific populations. It's no surprise, then, that facilities access (use of restrooms and locker rooms) is one of the most talked-about aspects of school life for gender-expansive people. Students of US and Canadian history will probably notice similarities between present-day debates and previous discourse around segregated schools, water fountains, restrooms, movie theaters, and other public spaces.

Restrooms are essential parts of daily school life for K–12 students. Locker rooms are commonly used facilities too. Students' experiences in these spaces affect their belonging and safety. Facilities access (or lack thereof) impacts their ability to benefit from the education provided at school. Inclusive policies on facilities access offer schools an opportunity to send a clear message of support and safety to their gender-expansive students and staff.

Access to Facilities That Match Gender Identity

Happy and healthy kids have access to facilities that match their gender identity. In theory, federal guidelines and state or provincial human rights laws protect gender-expansive students' rights to use those facilities. However, many schools struggle to implement those guidelines.

Unfortunately, restrooms and locker rooms are often hostile for LGBTQ+ students. Less than half of gender-expansive young people in the United States are able to use facilities that match their gender identity (Goldberg et al. 2023). As of May 2024, ten US states had banned transgender students from accessing the appropriate facilities, and three had laws or policies defining the word *sex* in a way that permits discrimination against transgender people (Movement Advancement Project 2024). Because of such hostility, some kids avoid using facilities for the entire school day. Many transgender students restrict food and liquid intake during the school day so they can avoid using the restroom, and because of this avoidance, trans kids are at increased risk for urinary tract infections and constipation (Henry 2019; Compton 2017). Anxiety around facilities use takes up valuable brain space and energy that could be better spent on learning. Deliberate separation or exclusion from facilities puts gender-expansive students at increased risk for anxiety, depression, and feelings of isolation, which in turn exacerbate gender dysphoria (Wernick, Kulick, and Chin 2017; Price-Feeney, Green, and Dorison 2021; Weinhardt et al. 2017). Gender dysphoria is distress arising from conflict between gender identity and sex assigned at birth.

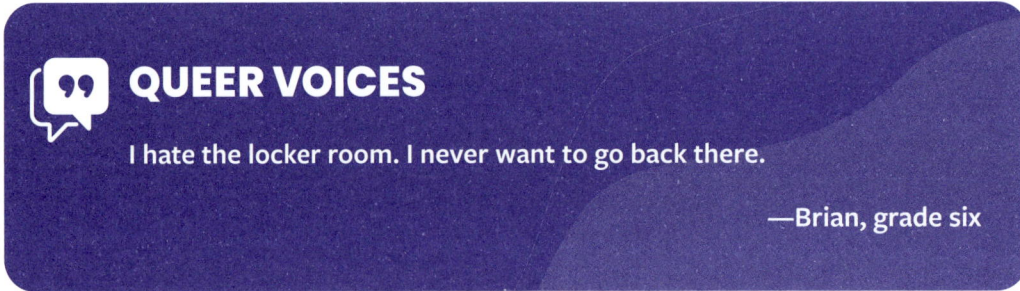

QUEER VOICES

I hate the locker room. I never want to go back there.

—Brian, grade six

Inclusion has the opposite effect. Evidence shows that inclusive policies increase positive student outcomes. Schools with inclusive policies enumerating protections for various populations see less bullying than those that don't have such policies (Hatzenbuehler and Keyes 2013; Kull et al. 2016). Centering student success should be the basis of decision making on facilities access.

Many organizations, including Gender Inclusive Schools, are advocating to further codify and guarantee inclusive access to school facilities for gender-expansive students. Meanwhile, schools can take practical steps to support happy and healthy kids and to protect their privacy and confidentiality.

Acknowledging Cis/Heteronormativity

In many schools, restrooms and locker rooms are separated by the gender binary into two options: male and female. This system reinforces cisgender and heterosexual people as the norm (cis/heteronormativity). Separating people in this way in places of undress implies that people can be only male or female as assigned at birth, and that people can be attracted only to the "opposite" gender.

I remember being told that "nudity in the locker room is no big deal because we are all boys." This kind of thinking is rife with stereotypes and gender/sexuality bias. The statement assumes that all the students in question are cisgender and straight. But there were almost certainly boys in the locker room whose sexual orientation meant that they were capable of attraction to the other boys changing around them. There were also trans girls and nonbinary kids intermingled in that same locker room, though it wasn't safe for them to be open about their identities. If behavior is the concern, the focus should be on what safety feels like in these spaces and how to encourage that behavior.

I encourage you to think about your assumptions—especially the assumption that everyone is cisgender and heterosexual by default, and assumptions you may make about safety and behavior based on cis/heteronormativity. At what point does a person's gender expression make you draw conclusions about their presence in a binary space? Does uncertainty about another person's gender make you feel unsafe or worried? Why? How would you feel if you thought everyone believed you shouldn't be in any space you used?

In addition to examining your assumptions, I encourage you to think about the daily experiences of gender-expansive students in your school. Take some time to walk around your building. Read posters, signs, and announcements as you go. Surf the school website and any digital learning platforms or school social media pages too. Take note of everything you see, hear, read, or navigate that reinforces a gender binary or heteronormativity. For example: What do your restrooms and locker rooms communicate? What spaces are free of binary norms? What does it mean to include people without a clearly defined gender or sexual orientation? This kind of inclusion walk can be done for any group of underrepresented student populations.

Invite colleagues to do the same exercise and compare notes. If possible, do a similar walk at another time of day or year.

Enhanced Privacy Options

An unfortunate and pervasive societal obsession with trans bodies contributes to hostile experiences for gender-expansive students when they need to access basic facilities at school. Showing one's body to classmates should never be a mandatory component of education. Furthermore, disclosing what one's body looks like, or what parts it has, to school staff has never been—and should never be—a requirement for entry into restrooms and locker rooms.

Enhanced privacy options for restrooms and locker rooms should be available for all members of a school community. Schools don't need to establish "allowable" justifications for this accommodation. People who ask for more privacy deserve access to more privacy. The reason behind their request is immaterial. Adding enhanced privacy options can happen even if no one is requesting it. Everyone is safest when people have healthy options and agency over their own bodies and privacy.

Enhanced privacy options should be available to all students, but should not be mandatory for any students. Forcing a gender-expansive student to use a separate facility is a form of exclusion. It puts the burden of accommodation on the marginalized student. Another student's discomfort about sharing space with a gender-expansive student cannot justify exclusion. If a student is uncomfortable changing in a locker room with a trans person, then they need to use the enhanced privacy option.

Restrooms

Many schools are finding success in serving all their students by following Universal Design principles to create equitable environments. That is: they make sure that environments are usable by all people, to the greatest extent possible, without adaptation. For restrooms, single-occupant unisex facilities or unisex restrooms with lockable floor-to-ceiling stalls are the most equitable and inclusive choice because they serve students with a wide range of abilities and needs. (For comprehensive information on the design, construction, and cost of inclusive restrooms, see "Inclusive Restroom Design Guide" on page 118.) You'll know that your facilities follow best practice when none of your students need to ask for special considerations or must endure uncomfortable situations or exclusion. Inclusion of the many types of individuals who benefit from easier access and increased privacy is an opportunity, not a burden.

QUEER VOICES

Gender-neutral bathrooms are the only bathrooms at my school. They are disgusting, but not any more disgusting than any other bathrooms.

—Dereke, grade eleven

Class restroom breaks are a necessary and routine part of the school day in many elementary schools, but this routine need not be a gender showcase. It is common for elementary students to line up as boys and girls for breaks. This habit compels students to publicly declare their gender multiple times a day. When binary restrooms are the only option, best practice is for all students to line up together. The teacher tells students how many people are allowed in the restroom at one time and says, "Wait until there is space available in the restroom that's best for you." This minimizes unnecessary and unwanted attention on gender-expansive students.

Locker Rooms

Enhancing privacy in locker rooms and changing facilities can mean building individual changing stalls. However, other less-expensive options work just as well. For example, a school could install privacy curtains, provide pop-up changing tents such as those used in theaters and at summer camps, or allow access to bathroom stalls with added time to dress for activities.

Inclusion can take additional time. Locker-room accommodations sometimes require a mindset shift, because they may eat into already limited instructional time. This time investment is worth it in the long run. For students to actively participate in and focus on physical education and health content, they must first feel safe entering and exiting locker rooms. Students who are terrified cannot receive the instruction provided by their educators. Allowing for safety and privacy in changing facilities positively impacts student learning.

💬 QUEER VOICES

My school put up curtains for changing, which I appreciated, but it still felt weird. If we had the same stalls in the locker rooms that we have in our gender-neutral bathrooms, it would be so much easier to feel comfortable.

—Sean, grade six

Schools Located under Hostile Laws and Restrictions

Ignoring the consensus among educational, medical, and psychological professional organizations, lawmakers in some areas have prioritized discriminatory belief systems above happy and healthy students. If you are an educator in a state or province with restrictive laws targeting transgender students in public schools, discrimination may be common and following best practices may be impossible. But the gender-expansive students in your school still need affirming educators. Be prepared to have honest conversations with LGBTQ+ students and acknowledge the harm they are enduring.

Ask yourself what actions will most benefit your students, what risks you are willing (or able) to take, and what steps you could follow to protect yourself personally and professionally in order to advocate for your students. Make sure your LGBTQ+ students know that the discrimination they are facing is unacceptable. Promise to do everything you can to support and affirm them despite the injustice.

Acknowledge the injustice and its impact. Naming discrimination is important, even when you can't fix it. There is nothing more frustrating for young people than adults invalidating harm while it's happening. Pretending it isn't happening makes the situation worse.

Guiding Principles Check-In

Support Happy and Healthy Kids: Existing in restrooms and locker rooms safely is foundational to successful participation at school. Full participation at school means being able to stay hydrated and sustained with breakfast and lunch, and using the restroom when needed. If your school has classes that require changing into sports attire, best practice for happy and healthy kids means not making gender-expansive kids think about their gender any more or less than cisgender kids when they're using restrooms and locker rooms.

Protect Privacy and Confidentiality: Information about the facilities a student uses at school is protected medical data. School staff should not be sharing or discussing this information unless they have a compelling reason to do so. Non-staff adults have no right to know which child is using which facility. Staff who share this information without consent are breaching educational privacy.

Responding to Challenging Questions and Comments

Challenge: *"So a student can just go in whatever bathroom they want? How will we know if someone is supposed to be in there?"*

Response: "It's not our job as teachers to decide if any student is in the correct bathroom. If a specific incident occurs related to student safety, please direct your concerns to the admin team."

Challenge: *"Are we going to just let boys run into the girls' restroom and not say anything?"*

Response: "If any student is entering the restroom for reasons other than to use the facilities, they aren't meeting expectations for acceptable behavior at school. We have instructed our students to use the facilities that match their gender identity, and if some students are not following those guidelines, please let us know. Students know that if they are using a facility as a joke, or to make someone else uncomfortable, they can expect a conversation with staff and their parents or caregivers."

Challenge: *"I hear there is a boy in the girls' bathroom with my daughter."*

Response: "All students at our school use the restrooms that best fit their needs and identities. We don't honor requests to keep specific students out of bathrooms, but we do have an all-gender restroom available for any student who asks for more privacy. Your daughter is welcome to use this option if she feels uncomfortable."

Response: "Everyone at our school is using the bathroom that is best for their learning and safety. We don't share information about where any of our students use the bathroom, just as I wouldn't share private information about your child."

Response: "What does your child need to feel safe using the bathroom at school?"

Challenge: *"The safety of women and girls is more important than letting transgender people access the facilities that match their gender identity."*

Response: "There is no association between equitable access to facilities and violent crime against women and girls. In fact, transgender people are 2.5 times more likely to be the victims of violent crime than cisgender people are" (Truman and Morgan 2022).

Response: "Our school district does not distinguish among genders when making decisions about binary facilities access. All students, including trans boys, trans girls, and nonbinary kids, have equal rights to safety and to access the facilities that match their gender identity in our schools."

Response: "No one in our community has a right to use facilities free from the presence of a protected class of people."

Challenge: *"I don't want my daughter exposed to that anatomy in the bathroom."*

Response: "We encourage all our students to use the restroom in a way that doesn't expose body parts. Is there a specific instance you are referring to, or are we talking about a hypothetical?"

Response: "If any of our students are exposing their body parts to others while using the restroom, then they are not meeting our behavior expectations. Is there a specific time or instance that made your child feel uncomfortable?"

Challenge: *"Transgender kids aren't going to be able to shower in the locker room, right?"*

Response: "I don't answer questions from community members about where any of our students use the bathroom or shower. All our students receive instruction on modest and appropriate behavior in our locker rooms. We have enhanced privacy options for any student who would like to access them."

Review and Reflection

Educational best practice is for gender-expansive students to use facilities that match their gender identity at school. The guiding principles of supporting happy and healthy kids and protecting privacy and confidentiality necessitate access to these facilities. But budget and space restrictions can make supplying that access difficult, especially on a short timeline. To overcome such difficulties, I encourage you to study other settings that have provided inclusive facilities for at least five years. Speak to the administrators.

Speak to the local LGBTQ+ youth-serving organizations and listen to their experiences. What hypothetical problems actually became issues as inclusive policies were implemented? How has inclusive access influenced student behavior and academic outcomes?

Assumptions and hypotheticals are often different from reality. If the gender hysteria often on display at school board meetings and in discriminatory legislation were based on reality, there would be massive behavioral and academic discrepancies between schools that have inclusive policies and schools that don't. In my experience working with hundreds of school communities, I've encountered only a handful of minor concerns related to LGBTQ+ student behavior in restrooms and locker rooms. Although isolated incidents do happen, the overwhelming majority of gender-expansive students try hard not to draw attention to themselves in restrooms and locker rooms. It would benefit most school communities to ignore hypothetical debates that demonize gender-expansive students and instead focus on problems that are actually happening.

To reflect on what is actually happening at your school, see the forms What Is "Normal" at Your School? and Behavioral Problem Areas at School on the following pages.

What Is "Normal" at Your School?

Gather a small group of colleagues to engage in a learning walk. As you move around the building in your school community, take notice of indicators that suggest to students that cisgender and heterosexual people are "normal" and everyone else is "different." Does the visual and spatial organization of your school communicate cis/heteronormativity? In what ways? Use the following prompts to gather information and reflect on what you find.

What does your school visually and functionally communicate as "normal" related to gender and sexual orientation throughout your school campus? List all the instances you notice, paying attention to signage, classroom organization, content in the library and on the walls, and the facilities that your students use on a regular basis.

After your learning walk, think and talk about the following questions:

- Were you aware of all of the situations you listed before engaging in this walk? Were they things you thought of on a day-to-day, regular basis?

- Which are easy to change? Which are hard?

- Which ones tell a counterstory? How many?

Behavioral Problem Areas at School

Following is a list of school locations where student behavior is often a concern. Next to each location, place an X for each serious incident you remember happening during the past two school years (requiring significant intervention by school staff).

classroom _____

hallway _____

lunchroom _____

bus/transportation _____

locker room _____

restroom _____

auditorium/assembly _____

athletic event _____

fine arts performance _____

library _____

gym _____

outside school _____

What do you notice about the locations in the school where student behavior required adult intervention? How do the incidents in restrooms and locker rooms compare to incidents in other locations? If there were incidents in restrooms and locker rooms, was a student's LGBTQ+ identity a contributing factor? Were these events related to inclusive access to facilities?

CHAPTER 6

Sports and Activities

Sports and extracurricular activities play a significant role in the school experiences of many students, including gender-expansive young people. Gender-expansive students are happier and healthier when they have access to the full spectrum of sports and activities offered by their school community (Clark and Kosciw 2020). It is educational best practice for a gender-expansive student to participate with the team or peer grouping that best fits their gender identity and their safety needs.

QUEER VOICES

It's not even a big deal. I don't think anyone really cares which team I play on, and I've been a girl forever. It would be so weird for me to play on a different team, no one would understand. It was always just like, duh, of course I'll be on the girls' team. No one had any questions.

—Wren, grade eight

Sports

More than 80 percent of transgender young people participating on sports teams do not disclose their LGBTQ+ status to their coaches (Richards 2023). For many kids, sacrificing their authenticity is worth it if it provides them an opportunity to play. It speaks to the importance of sport for many queer young people that they will silently endure homophobia and transphobia if they can be part of a team. Some trans youth delay or avoid social transitions so they can continue participating on the team that matches their sex assigned at birth, and some trans youth do not disclose their trans identity so they can safely play on the team that matches their gender identity. As a parent of a transgender child, I'm heartbroken to imagine her being forced to pretend she's someone she isn't just to be included in an activity that's important to her.

School sports participation for gender-expansive students depends largely on the governing bodies of state athletic associations. In the United States, new Title IX rules expand the definition of sex discrimination to include gender identity but do not specifically address transgender athletes' participation in sports (Stanford 2024). Local regulations don't always align with federal guidance that protects students from sex discrimination. Recent legislation in some US states and Canadian provinces makes it illegal for transgender students to access the same opportunities offered to their peers. Bans on transgender athletes send a clear and harmful message to all young people: *the world of sports, with all of its benefits and celebrations, is not for you.*

QUEER VOICES

The boys' and girls' cross country teams practice together. As a nonbinary athlete, it feels good to just be a runner during practice, even if I still have to compete in gendered races.

—Mel, grade ten

The case of Mack Beggs, a transgender man, highlights the predicament trans athletes find themselves in while competing in states with trans athlete bans. In 2017, while Mack was in high school, he won the Texas state girls' wrestling championship for his weight class to a mixed chorus of boos and cheers. The policy of the University Interscholastic League, which oversees school sports in Texas, is to determine athletes' gender by their birth certificates. Despite being a transgender boy taking testosterone and requesting to compete in the boys' division, Mack was forced to compete against girls (Payne 2017).

School staff should plan on following the legal limitations on their school community while acknowledging how inequities and discriminatory policies affect students. A gender-inclusive school will also work hard to advocate against discriminatory laws and find ways to support and protect its gender-expansive students. If changing or working around the law is not immediately possible, school leaders and staff must speak up about the impacts of the law. When communities throw up their hands in defeat and say things like, "There's nothing we can do," or, "It's not up to me," without naming the harm that discrimination causes, trans students hear, "You're not worth the effort."

How is your school community shining a light on discriminatory laws and making the negative impact on students visible? How are you communicating your students' needs and their discomfort to decision makers in your community? It's not enough to exist silently within systems of oppression. Educators must always advocate for best practices.

Policies on the participation of transgender students in sports are commonly acknowledged in a school's gender-inclusion policy, then spelled out fully within the athletic governing bodies' policies. For positive examples of high school athletic association guidance on the participation of transgender students in sports, visit transathlete.com, click on Policies/North America/High School Policies, and review the "friendly" state and provincial guidelines.

Activities

Like sports, nonathletic activities should allow gender-expansive students to participate in ways that honor who they know themselves to be. Most schools find it fairly easy to offer gender-inclusive nonathletic activities such as choir, band, orchestra, theater, student council, student clubs, and affinity groups.

Fine arts and other activities involving self-expression have long been havens for LGBTQ+ people. Theater in particular provides wonderful opportunities for students to explore and embody characters of various genders and identities. More and more schools are labeling characters and roles in productions as masculine and feminine instead of male and female. Similarly, voice parts in musicals or choirs can simply list the voice range required.

Many school traditions, especially at the high school level, are rigidly gendered. Taking binary gender norms out of school traditions may feel like a big change for some school communities. Even small changes to traditions, like naming homecoming or prom "royalty" instead of "king and queen," can inspire vocal pushback. But it's possible to make school traditions welcoming and open to all students without changing their core purpose. For most schools, the function of such traditions is to celebrate students who exemplify valued qualities that make them leaders and models for their peers.

Dress Codes

Think about areas in which your school rules might be reinforcing binary gender norms or creating unnecessary discomfort for your gender-expansive students. Schoolwide dress codes are a common problem area. Dress codes should be stated and enforced in gender-neutral ways. Items of clothing required to participate in sports or activities should also be gender inclusive. For example, instead of providing a list of gendered expectations for student dress at an upcoming band concert, educators should list all acceptable items of clothing and allow students to choose the garments that are best for them. Likewise, performances, graduation ceremonies, and milestone events such as homecoming and prom should all have gender-neutral expectations for student dress.

Following Students into the Future

Allowing students to drive the process of improving gender inclusion at school is both empowering and powerful. When adults are following student-led self-advocacy initiatives, it is harder for decision makers to throw up roadblocks—and the intitiatives represent what students actually want and need. Working with your school's Genders and Sexualities Alliance (GSA) or LGBTQ+ affinity group is often the first step in pursuing meaningful change. Even if these groups don't exist at your school, you can still follow the lead of your students and support their efforts.

Student leadership can look like the following:

- **Student-led training:** Students can create and lead training for staff, planning committees, homeroom or advisory classes, or the school board on practices students believe should be changed, added, or removed—as well as the impact of those practices.

- **Student activism:** From walkouts to teach-ins, from days of silence to days of protest, from letter writing to hashtagging, students can take a variety of proactive and reactive actions to make themselves heard. They deserve a voice in their community.

- **Event planning:** When a specific school event needs improvement, students can have input by joining the planning committee for that event. Students can also host alternative, more inclusive, events outside the school.

QUEER VOICES

My high school is in a small town, about three thousand people. Having a homecoming king and queen was really important. They led the parade on Main Street every year, and people remembered [hearing about] their parents and grandparents being crowned. But our class had the first student council to decide not to specify gender for these positions. Starting last year, we just called them homecoming royalty. We had seen other schools do similar things, and several years earlier people were mad that a transgender student was on the ballot in a category that matched her gender. There weren't any school policies or rules from the school board, so our student government just made the change. People were upset, but what are they going to do? We are the ones deciding which students represent our school on this important day, and we don't need one "boy" and one "girl" to do that.

—Raven, age seventeen (they/them)

- **Peer support:** Members of marginalized communities often feel as if they are fighting alone for their rights. Student leaders who are not part of those communities can have a huge impact on the climate and culture of a school when they work to support their marginalized classmates.

Guiding Principles Check-In

Support Happy and Healthy Kids: Sports and activities offer students opportunities beyond the academic day to find fulfillment and camaraderie. It's a well-known best practice to encourage students to pursue passions in athletics, arts, sciences, and other areas that help them develop the skills they need to be contributing members of society. If sports and activities are educational best practice for cisgender students, then they are also best practice for gender-expansive students. Schools can increase involvement in these opportunities by reducing barriers to participation.

Protect Privacy and Confidentiality: Students must be able to participate in sports and activities in ways that respect their right to control information about their gender identity. Some schools are trampling on the privacy of all students in an effort to exclude gender-expansive students from athletics. For example, many local governing bodies' guidelines use language such as "sex on a student's original birth certificate." Schools must operate in accordance with the requirements of the governing associations, but make no mistake: it is best practice for students to not be asked or forced to disclose information about their bodies in order to participate on the team that matches their gender identity.

Responding to Challenging Questions and Comments

Challenge: *"I don't want my daughter competing against boys. It's unsafe."*

Response: "Some states and provinces have had gender-inclusive athletic policies for a decade, and zero injuries related to your concerns have been reported. We have no reason to believe that our school community's athletics will be any different from those serving millions of students across the continent."

Challenge: *"It's just not fair that my daughter will lose out on an opportunity because of a transgender girl."*

Response: "Is this a hypothetical situation, or do you have a specific concern your athlete needs addressing this season?"

Challenge: *"Boys and girls are just biologically different, and we shouldn't be allowing these sex differences to give one person an advantage."*

Response (long version): "The concept of advantage in sports is complicated. A wide variety of biological differences give some individuals advantages when they compete. This spectrum of difference includes physical size, metabolic rates, hormone production, body types, and physical shape. These differences can contribute to exceptional athletic performance. However, we do not exclude the extremes of these differences for cisgender athletes. For example, we don't test high school cisgender boys' testosterone production to determine if they have an unfair advantage on the football field. There is no data showing the impact of a student's trans identity is more or less significant than any of these other naturally occurring differences that represent the breadth of human diversity."

Response (short version): "Our teams follow the guidelines offered by our state athletic association. If you have a concern about athletic participation for your child, please reach out to their governing board."

Challenge: *"Can't we just have a team just for the transgender students?"*

Response: "Most of our student athletes will not pursue competitive sports as their vocation later in life. Opportunities to participate on a team and pursue common goals are good for the psychological and social development of all students, and best practice for all students is to allow them to learn and grow in an inclusive environment."

Response: "Facilitating segregated student programming goes against our values of justice and community."

Challenge: *"We've always had a homecoming king and queen. Why should we have to change our traditions to be more 'woke?'"*

Response: "Traditions evolve over time. Our student body voted overwhelmingly to recognize homecoming royalty in a gender-neutral way at our homecoming celebration. We are thrilled to honor their wishes to be more inclusive."

Review and Reflection

While decisions regarding trans athletes' participation in sports are usually controlled by entities outside a school, schools can still work toward doing what is best for happy and healthy students by centering their needs—regardless of circumstance. When possible, activities and sports at school should be available to students of all genders equitably. Exploring career paths, engaging in self-expression, and practicing skills through sports and activities are important ways of developing a sense of purpose and identity.

The following activity focuses on sports and gender. I've found that many people have strong opinions about the participation of transgender people in sports. But there is often a disconnect between their stated opinions and their day-to-day relationships with sports—especially women's athletics. Engage with the Sports and Gender form individually before discussing your answers with a friend or colleague.

Sports and Gender

Without using your phone or computer to look things up, see if you can fill in the information requested below.

Name the first and last names of three transgender athletes competing in your state or province.

Name two transgender people who have competed in the Olympics.

List five professional women's sports teams.

List five professional athletes you went to high school with.

With a partner or colleague, discuss what you can learn from your responses. Here are a few questions to get you started:

- How large of a role do transgender athletes currently play in your experience with sports you or your family follow or participate in?

- What does society's collective knowledge of women's sports in general say about its focus on trans girls being part of athletic teams?

- Do you see a disconnect between societal perceptions and on-the-ground realities in sports?

- If you were a trans student athlete, how would you feel knowing that the adult decision makers regulating your participation in sports might not know any trans people personally?

- If you were a trans student athlete, how would it feel to have your participation in sports be a common topic of debate?

CHAPTER 7

Names and Pronouns

People whose names or pronouns given at birth don't match their gender identity often decide to move through the world with new names and/or pronouns. As an educator, you have the honor of watching young people develop into their full selves over time. This means that you may have the privilege of supporting students through changes in their names and pronouns.

It's basic human decency to use the language someone asks you to use when referring to them. Has someone ever introduced themself to you and you replied, "I'm not going to call you that"? Of course not. When people tell you who they are, you don't ask questions about their birth, their legal documents, and their history in the world. This chapter explains how to affirm students' names and pronouns and how to navigate mistakes simply and respectfully.

> ## 💬 QUEER VOICES
>
> When I told my teachers I wanted to be called Scout, it was super easy. They even asked me if it was okay to put my chosen name in the band program, or if I wanted to do something different.
>
> —Scout, grade six

Names

After a student socially transitions—and sometimes before, as they are exploring their gender—the student may begin using a new name. You should always use the names students ask you to use, unless a name disrupts learning. Students should not be required to change their official school records or engage in a legal process to have their names respected in school communications, IDs, lockers, attendance documents, or other daily uses.

It is common for students to adopt multiple new names, sometimes returning to previously used names, over the course of their time in school. These are developmentally appropriate and expected changes as students explore their identities. Follow a student's lead when they first change their name. Your goal should be to minimize mistakes and maximize affirmation.

When students make frequent name changes, more frequent mistakes will logically follow. You can support these students by developing affirming communication habits. Find ways to do quick, private check-ins, saying something like, "Hey, still using (name)?" After you receive new information from a student, moving forward together to the best of your ability is all anyone can ask for.

Pronouns

Most people feel comfortable with others using pronouns in place of their name in conversation and in writing. The following chart offers some pronoun examples. Some nonbinary people use they/them pronouns, and many students also use pronoun combinations like she/they. One-fourth of LGBTQ+ youth use pronouns outside the binary of he/him and she/her (Trevor Project 2020).

Pronoun Examples

Subjective Pronoun	Objective Pronoun	Possessive Adjective	Possessive Pronoun	Reflexive Pronoun
He (He made cupcakes.)	Him (I thanked him.)	His (His cupcakes are delicious.)	His (That recipe is his.)	Himself (He created the recipe himself.)
She	Her	Her	Hers	Herself
Fae ("fay")	Faer ("fair")	Faer ("fair")	Faers ("fairs")	Faerself ("fairself")
Ze ("zee")	Zir ("zeer")	Zir ("zeer")	Zirs ("zeers")	Zirself ("zeerself")
They	Them	Their	Theirs	Themself

Many cisgender people have never given serious thought to pronouns. However, most cisgender people have strong reactions when an incorrect pronoun is used for them or someone they know. The same is true for gender-expansive people. Being called by the correct pronouns is a basic respect that every person deserves. Inclusive pronoun use allows all members of a school community to learn and work in an environment where they can control how they are treated with language.

QUEER VOICES

My teacher asked me what name I wanted to use in class on the first day. It made me feel welcome, like my name wasn't a big deal for her to use.

—Brianne, grade four

Exploring Fit

The decision to explore new names or pronouns is entirely dependent on the individual. People often change names and pronouns at the same time during a social transition. Students may begin trying on new names and pronouns to see what fits their internal sense of self—boy, girl, a blend of both, or neither.

Student changes in names and pronouns usually require some active learning on the part of their educators. This new learning shouldn't come as a surprise or be seen as a burden. After all, good educators are lifelong learners.

If you have worked in a school at any point during the last several years, you've probably known of at least one student who changed their name and/or pronouns. And if that's the case, I bet you've also gotten a student's name or pronouns wrong at least once. Using new names and pronouns can be a challenge at first, especially with a student you've known for a long time. But it's important to keep trying, and it gets easier with practice. Using the correct name and pronouns is a small effort teachers can make that has a big positive impact on a student's school experience.

At the end of this chapter, you will find forms for use during open houses and the first days of class. These forms can help you, your fellow educators, and families use inclusive and affirming language to address and refer to your students, regardless of their age.

- **Student Information Sheet:** Use this form with middle or high school students at the beginning of the school year or term or when a new student joins your class. You can either use a hard copy or email it to students. The form allows students to privately share information about the name they would like to be called in class and the pronouns they would like you to use, as well as what names and pronouns they would like you to use with parents, caregivers, family members, other school staff, and classmates. You can also use this form to gather information about how to pronounce your students' names, whether they use nicknames, or if there is anything else you need to know to support them in their learning. All students benefit from being able to share the language and words that make them feel safe at school.

- **Name and Pronouns Educator Affirmation:** This tool can help you practice using a student's new name and pronouns following a social transition or using a set of pronouns new to you, such as they/them or fae/faer.

- **Name and Pronouns Family Affirmation:** This tool can help families practice using their family members' names and pronouns in a way that centers love and belonging.

- **Pronoun Practice: Family or Educator Story:** Sometimes families or staff need a bit of guided practice. These forms help adults practice using a student's names and pronouns in the context of a social story.

- **Pronoun Practice: Family Discussion Prompts:** Using the correct name and pronoun for someone is important even when they aren't present. This form gives family members prompts for having a discussion about their child to practice using their affirmed name and pronouns.

There are times when directly asking a student what pronouns they use isn't feasible or could draw unwanted attention to their gender identity. I've watched well-meaning educators drop everything and do a pronoun-go-round once they notice that one of their students is gender-expansive. While the intention behind this type of action is important, the execution doesn't follow the principle of protecting privacy and confidentiality. Be aware of the audience for your questions and whether the setting allows students to control how they share information about their gender identities with their classmates, other educators, or community members.

Adaptations for Younger Students

At almost every primary school training I facilitate, the question of age-appropriateness comes up related to names and pronouns. I hear comments like, "We don't even learn about pronouns until sixth grade" and, "Aren't they too young to be changing pronouns?" In actuality, pronouns offer a powerful springboard to understanding. While a five-year-old might not grasp the grammatical concept of pronouns, they absolutely understand the concept of what feels right and what feels wrong. If you were to ask a cisgender five-year-old boy if you could call him "she," he would probably have a strong reaction. If you were to ask him if the pronoun *she* felt right or wrong to him, he would say emphatically, "Wrong." This concept of wrong-ness is easy for young children to understand and can serve as a bridge to empathy and understanding when a classmate changes pronouns during the school year. Young children can understand that it's not okay to use the old pronoun because it feels wrong, just as using incorrect binary pronouns for them feels wrong.

For students in preK through fifth grade, you can adapt the ideas in the Student Information Sheet to be developmentally and functionally appropriate. Adding text to an open-house form, or verbally checking in with students at the beginning of the year, allows younger children and their families to easily share information about names and pronouns. For example, you could add the following sentences to an open-house form: *What name would your child liked to be called in class this school year? What pronouns will they be using?* This approach accommodates all students whose registration names don't match the names they use every day. It also sets the expectation that all community members will show respect by using the names and pronouns students use.

Doing Better Every Day

You're human, so you're going to make mistakes with student names and pronouns. Mistakes are an inevitable part of supporting students who socially transition at school. Forgive yourself and others for inadvertent errors, but do not permit any staff member to persistently or purposefully deadname others. (To deadname is to use a name previously associated with someone's incorrect gender identity.) Schools should handle intentional misgendering and deadnaming as harassment under student and staff behavioral agreements.

When I discuss name and pronoun mistakes during trainings across North America, I often hear from parents, caregivers, and educators that "this is just so new to me," "I've always thought of *they* as meaning multiple people," and other comments that center themselves. They focus on their own discomfort or difficulty instead of the harm to gender-expansive students of misgendering and/or deadnaming them. To avoid compounding the harm when you make a mistake, remember this simple fact: it's not about you.

When you make a mistake, follow these best practices:

1. **Say, "Thank you" instead of "I'm sorry."** When you thank a student for correcting you, you communicate that you didn't want to make the mistake, and you want them to keep correcting you if you make a mistake again. Educators sometimes overapologize, even burst into tears, following a mistake. It does feel bad to have said something you know might hurt someone, but it is important not to display your regret so dramatically that the person you harmed feels like they must comfort you. Don't make it about you.

2. **Repeat the sentence using the correct name and/or pronoun.** If you said, "She's in the library" about someone who uses they/them pronouns, correct yourself by saying, "They're in the library." When you follow up by speaking the correct language out loud, it's the last thing you think about—and this helps you do better next time.

3. **Do better.** Your commitment to inclusion isn't measured by getting things right 100 percent of the time. However, gender-expansive students can reasonably expect that their educators will improve over time. Keep asking yourself: "Am I making fewer mistakes today than I did yesterday?" Showing someone that their well-being is worth your personal growth is a powerful demonstration of support.

4. **Practice.** If you (or your school community) aren't doing better over time, something needs to change. Often, persistent mistakes happen when adults are not interacting regularly with the student in question. Practicing someone's name and pronouns away from that person is an effective way to minimize future mistakes. Using the forms at the end of this chapter is a great way to start.

Guiding Principles Check-In

Support Happy and Healthy Kids: Students are happiest and healthiest when their identities are congruent across all the environments they exist in. Young people deserve to be their authentic selves at home, at school, in their faith communities, with their extended families, and elsewhere in their lives. In fact, positive mental health outcomes increase exponentially as the number of settings in which names and pronouns are respected increases (Russell et al. 2018).

Protect Privacy and Confidentiality: It is educational best practice to let students control the timing and manner of disclosing their identity to others in a school community. Schools should not develop policies that automatically notify parents and caregivers when their students use new names or pronouns. Forced disclosure is dangerous in instances where students experience physical and/or emotional harm when outed to their parents without their consent. Gender-expansive students face disproportionate levels of abuse within their families (Thoma et al. 2021). You can never truly know the full circumstances of what your students experience at home, so follow their lead on whether it is safe for them to share information about their gender identity with their families.

It's important to know what each student is comfortable with. If a student is using the same name and pronouns everywhere and with everyone at school, it is safe—and can be helpful—to correct mistakes and practice together during staff meetings and conversations. But sometimes students transition only in specific places or with specific people. Communicate safely and effectively with and about students to respect their privacy.

Responding to Challenging Questions and Comments

Challenge: *"I've been using he/him and she/her pronouns for fifty years, and I'm not going to change now."*

Response: "Sometimes we need to grow and learn to make sure that other groups of people are valued, seen, and included in our schools. We expect everyone in our school community to use the language others ask us to use to describe who they are."

Challenge: *"What if a child says they are a giraffe? Am I supposed to respect that too?"*

Response: "Are we talking about something you have actually observed or a hypothetical situation?"

Response: "Gender identity is who a person knows themself to be—boy, girl, a blend of both, or neither. Identifying as an animal is something else entirely and not part of this conversation."

Response: "Making LGBTQ+ identities a joke by equating them to animals minimizes the discrimination LGBTQ+ people face every day. Our school will not entertain such conversations because they cause real harm to members of our community."

Challenge: *"I won't lie. I'm going to call people what they are. You can't make me use he/him pronouns for someone I know is really a girl."*

Response: "Our school staff come from a variety of backgrounds and hold many different beliefs in their private lives. However, the expectations for staff behavior are the same for everyone: We use the names and pronouns our students ask us to use. If you can't meet that expectation, you will be subject to the same disciplinary action as you would for violating any of our other nondiscrimination guidelines."

Challenge: *"Why are they getting so mad when I make mistakes? I'm not perfect, and they need to calm down."*

Response: "When our students are experiencing harm, we never put the onus on them to make us feel better about our behavior. We understand that people will make mistakes. We also have a reasonable expectation that we staff will get better over time at using students' correct names and pronouns. Let me know if you need support or some ways to practice."

Review and Reflection

Affirming language is a prerequisite to productive learning relationships between students and educators at school. This chapter offers many practical suggestions for supporting students by using the names and pronouns they ask you to use. When you make mistakes, here's the best sequence of actions:

1. Say, "Thank you for correcting me."
2. Repeat the sentence using the correct name and/or pronouns.
3. Do better.
4. Practice with the resources at the end of this chapter.

Think about your own name and the pronouns that people use to describe you. Think back to your K–12 school experiences. How might your life have been different if everyone in your school community called you by a name and pronouns that didn't match who you are? What would it feel like to hear the wrong name or pronouns constantly in conversations? Hearing other people deny the reality of your existence and your relationships can be upsetting, distracting, demoralizing, infuriating, disrespectful, and damaging in many other ways. Gender-expansive students deserve the basic decency of being seen and referred to as who they are.

Student Information Sheet

Date _____

What is the name you want me to call you in class this school year?

What name should I use in front of other students?

What name should I use when I contact your parents or caregivers?

What name should I use with other teachers, including substitutes?

What are your pronouns? (for example: he/him/his, she/her/hers, they/them/theirs)

What pronouns should I use in front of other students?

What pronouns should I use when I contact your parents or caregivers?

What pronouns should I use with other teachers, including substitutes?

Is there anything else you would like me to know about using your name and pronouns?

Name and Pronouns
Educator Affirmation

This form is an opportunity to privately voice your commitment to using a student's affirmed name and pronouns while increasing your fluency and comfort with them. You can use it to practice after school, during your preparation period before you have the student in class, or after making a mistake. Practice makes progress! Try speaking the words two or three times in a row every morning. You will be surprised at how fluent you sound and feel after practicing.

Name: _____   Possessive adjective: _____

Subjective pronoun: _____   Possessive pronoun: _____

Objective pronoun: _____   Reflexive pronoun: _____

_____ (name) is awesome. _____ (subjective pronoun) is/are an amazing part of our school community. _____ (possesive adjective) life is important. I am going to get better at using _____ (possesive adjective) affirmed pronouns and _____ (possesive adjective) affirmed name. _____ (possesive adjective) identity is _____ (possessive pronoun), and I care about _____ (objective pronoun).

Pronoun Examples

Subjective Pronoun	Objective Pronoun	Possessive Adjective	Possessive Pronoun	Reflexive Pronoun
He (He made cupcakes.)	Him (I thanked him.)	His (His cupcakes are delicious.)	His (That recipe is his.)	Himself (He created the recipe himself.)
She	Her	Her	Hers	Herself
Fae	Faer	Faer	Faers	Faerself
Ze	Zir	Zir	Zirs	Zirself
They	Them	Their	Theirs	Themself

Name and Pronouns Family Affirmation

This form is an opportunity to privately voice your commitment to using your child's affirmed name and pronouns while increasing your fluency and comfort with them. You can use it to practice on your own, with other family members, before your child returns from school or an activity, or after you've made a mistake despite your best intentions. Practice makes progress! Try speaking the words two or three times in a row every morning. You will be surprised at how fluent you sound and feel after practicing.

Name: _____   Possessive adjective: _____

Subjective pronoun: _____   Possessive pronoun: _____

Objective pronoun: _____   Reflexive pronoun: _____

_____ (name) is awesome. _____ (subjective pronoun)

is/are an amazing part of our family. _____ (possesive adjective) life is important.

I am going to get better at using _____ (possesive adjective) affirmed pronouns

and _____ (possesive adjective) affirmed name. _____ (possesive adjective)

identity is _____ (possessive pronoun), and I love _____ (objective pronoun)

exactly the way _____ (subjective pronoun) is/are.

Pronoun Examples

Subjective Pronoun	Objective Pronoun	Possessive Adjective	Possessive Pronoun	Reflexive Pronoun
He (He made cupcakes.)	Him (I thanked him.)	His (His cupcakes are delicious.)	His (That recipe is his.)	Himself (He created the recipe himself.)
She	Her	Her	Hers	Herself
Fae	Faer	Faer	Faers	Faerself
Ze	Zir	Zir	Zirs	Zirself
They	Them	Their	Theirs	Themself

Pronoun Practice: Family Story

This form is an opportunity for extended practice with your child's name and pronouns. You can improve your conversational fluency by speaking your child's name and pronouns out loud in the context of a social story. Repeated practice can help you feel comfortable and prepared to talk about your child with others.

Name: _____   Possessive adjective: _____

Subjective pronoun: _____   Possessive pronoun: _____

Objective pronoun: _____   Reflexive pronoun: _____

Yesterday, I asked _____ (name) if _____ (subjective pronoun) wanted to go to the store. _____ (name) said _____ (subjective pronoun) would love to come with me, and asked if we could stop by another store too. When we left our house, I handed _____ (objective) the keys and _____ (subjective) locked the door while I started the car. _____ (name) realized that _____ (subjective pronoun) had forgotten _____ (possessive adjective) phone in the house, went back inside to get it from _____ (possessive adjective) room, and ran back to get in the car and buckle _____ (possessive adjective) seatbelt. While we were driving, I asked _____ (name) if _____ (subjective pronoun) had plans with _____ (possessive adjective) friends later that evening. _____ (subjective pronoun) said _____ (subjective pronoun) didn't really know yet. _____ (name) was waiting for a message back from a friend of _____ (possessive pronoun). I said _____ (subjective pronoun) could make the choice for _____ (reflexive pronoun), but that I would love to watch a movie with _____ (objective pronoun) later. We walked into the store together, did our shopping, and then I asked _____ (name) which store _____ (subjective pronoun) would like to go to next. _____ (subjective pronoun) said it didn't matter anymore, and that _____ (subjective pronoun) would rather just go home and hang out. We drove back home and _____ (name) helped me unload the bags from the car, and _____ (subjective) put them on the kitchen counter.

→

Pronoun Examples

Subjective Pronoun	Objective Pronoun	Possessive Adjective	Possessive Pronoun	Reflexive Pronoun
He (He made cupcakes.)	Him (I thanked him.)	His (His cupcakes are delicious.)	His (That recipe is his.)	Himself (He created the recipe himself.)
She	Her	Her	Hers	Herself
Fae	Faer	Faer	Faers	Faerself
Ze	Zir	Zir	Zirs	Zirself
They	Them	Their	Theirs	Themself

Gender-Inclusive Schools © David Edwards—Free Spirit Publishing

Pronoun Practice: Educator Story

This form is an opportunity for extended practice with a student's name and pronouns. You can improve your conversational fluency by speaking the student's name and pronouns out loud in the context of a classroom social story. Repeated practice can help you feel comfortable and prepared to use the language a student asks you to use at school.

Name: _____   Possessive adjective: _____

Subjective pronoun: _____   Possessive pronoun: _____

Objective pronoun: _____   Reflexive pronoun: _____

Yesterday, _____ (name) was late for class for the first time.

When _____ (subjective) walked in, I asked _____ (objective) what

happened. _____ (name) explained that _____ (subjective) had

dropped _____ (possessive pronoun) backpack in the hall and everything spilled

out. I asked if _____ (name) needed any help getting things

organized, and _____ (subjective) said _____ (subjective) could figure

it out _____ (reflexive). We started the day's lesson, and I placed the students

in collaborative learning groups. _____ (name) was in a group with

two other students. _____ (name) volunteered to pass out the note

cards and colored pencils we needed for the lesson, and _____ (subjective)

gave each group the materials. I thanked _____ (objective) for being willing

to help. The groups responded to the lesson prompts by writing on the note

cards. _____ (name) collected the note cards. When we

shifted to an independent writing activity, _____ (name) worked

at _____ (possessive adjective) desk until there were five minutes of class

left. I asked the students to pass their writing assignments forward for collection. Several

papers did not have student names on them. I asked _____ (name) if any

of those papers were _____ (possessive pronoun). _____ (name) said

that _____ (subjective) had written _____ (possessive adjective) name

on _____ (possessive adjective) paper.

→

Pronoun Examples

Subjective Pronoun	Objective Pronoun	Possessive Adjective	Possessive Pronoun	Reflexive Pronoun
He (He made cupcakes.)	Him (I thanked him.)	His (His cupcakes are delicious.)	His (That recipe is his.)	Himself (He created the recipe himself.)
She	Her	Her	Hers	Herself
Fae	Faer	Faer	Faers	Faerself
Ze	Zir	Zir	Zirs	Zirself
They	Them	Their	Theirs	Themself

Pronoun Practice:
Family Discussion Prompts

After using the Pronoun Practice: Family Story form, you may be ready to practice with fewer supports. Using the following prompts, talk about your child using their affirmed name and pronouns. Your child's gender identity is important, but it is not their entire identity. These prompts can help you have a conversation about your child's hopes and dreams, your shared experiences, their strengths and weaknesses, and other things that make them unique and amazing. If you find yourself making pronoun mistakes during regular conversations, this type of structured practice can help you reduce the harm of deadnaming and misgendering.

1. What do you think your child will do for a career after graduation or leaving home? What will your child need to do to achieve their goals?

2. What is your funniest memory of your young person? What makes it so memorable?

3. If your child could live in any city in the world, where would they go? Why?

4. Is your child a night owl or a morning person? How are they different from or similar to you in this regard?

5. What are some of your young person's most prized possessions or favorite things? Why do they care so much about these items?

6. What kinds of books, shows, or movies did your child enjoy when they were younger? How do those interests match up to what they enjoy today?

7. Is your young person more interested in academics/activities or in being social with friends? Has this shifted over time since your young person was little?

8. How does your child learn best? What are some things they need from educators to be successful?

9. What is your young person's most annoying habit? Why does it bother you so much?

10. What is your child's biggest strength? How did they get so strong in this area?

CHAPTER 8

Visible Support

How can you put into practice the caring, encouragement, and respect you feel for your LGBTQ+ students? How can you recognize the courage they show in being their authentic selves every day despite all the marginalization they experience? You can make your support visible so students know they are safe with you, so they know you won't judge them for their gender expression, and to counteract society's constant negativity. Visible support, affirmation, and LGBTQ+ representation across all facets of school—from Pride banners to posters that set expectations to queer people represented in lessons and curriculum—has an immediate positive impact. You can make your support visible in many ways; this chapter describes just a few. The ultimate goal is getting the thoughts in your brain into something tangible that LGBTQ+ students can interact with.

Visibility in Physical Spaces

Whenever I walk into a school building for the first time, I look for clues. That is: I note how long it takes to locate positive, inclusive messages. Many people from historically marginalized backgrounds do this routinely as a necessary safety practice.

As a queer person who has experienced discrimination growing up as a child at school, discrimination in college, and discrimination in the workplace, when I take my family to school I feel like I'm automatically on alert, maybe even on edge. After walking in with my kids, I search for clues that they are going to be safe and our family is going to be respected. That safe-space sticker might seem like a small deal to some people, but not to us. It's a signal that we can talk about who our family members are, openly and honestly.

How does the entrance to your school communicate inclusion of students from a variety of backgrounds, cultures, and identities? Visible signs of inclusivity don't have to be complicated or expensive. While affirming stickers, posters, banners, flags, and more are widely available for sale, homemade ones are just as impactful. Do what you can with the resources you have. When your students can see and hear your affirmation, they are more likely to show up at school ready to succeed academically and socially.

Do a few classrooms have safe-space stickers on their doors, or does every single classroom have one? A few teachers showing visible support is good, but all staff presenting a unified front is better. When one teacher explicitly supports all student identities, but other teachers are silent, passive, or neutral on the subject, LGBTQ+ students are left to fill in the information gap. They may wonder why—and feel stress from the uncertainty—or they may assume that the silent teachers are actively unsupportive or even hostile.

If you are reluctant to visibly support LGBTQ+ students, I encourage you to ask yourself why. What is stopping you from taking that step? Does the impact of your choice match the intent that you hold in your heart and mind?

Public educators have a responsibility to meet the needs of all students. All students have a right to learn in environments where the adults care about their success regardless of their identities. There's no exemption allowing educators to refuse to support students because student identities conflict with an educator's privately held beliefs. In places of public accommodation, school employees don't get to pick and choose which kinds of students they will support. Across all learning settings—including independent schools or other settings outside the purview of nondiscrimination laws—most teachers do not want to deliberately exclude or other a specific subset of their student populations.

Safe-Space Language

Safe-space language occasionally receives pushback because putting up a sticker or poster or wearing a badge doesn't magically prevent discrimination. Educators who mean well sometimes fall short of the values indicated by their visible signs of inclusivity. For example, a teacher with a Black Lives Matter sign on their door may still express racial bias either consciously or unconsciously, or a teacher with a Protect Trans Kids sticker on their water bottle may consistently forget a student's pronouns.

Visible signs of inclusivity are simply tools. How an educator uses those tools determines whether they aid or hinder the values they represent. One educator using a tool incorrectly doesn't prevent another educator from using the same tool successfully.

No educator can promise that their students will never encounter discrimination or harm at school. However, educators can respond to discrimination in ways that reduce harm and honor the dignity and value of every school community member. And there is great power in setting goals that allow students to succeed—and declaring those goals publicly. Declaring a safe space doesn't prevent bad things from happening. Rather, it reminds educators to proactively educate, competently respond to bias when it occurs, and unapologetically place the safety of students first.

Equitable Visibility

Equitable visibility means including the LGBTQ+ community in opportunities such as affinity groups and parent advisory committees just like those that are in place for students with disabilities, students of color, and students who speak languages other than English at home. Messages about the LGBTQ+ community must be celebratory and affirming, not just focused on the impact of historical marginalization. When we enrolled our middle schooler in our neighborhood school district, my wife and I entered the terms *LGBTQ*, *gay*, and *transgender* in the district search bar. The only result for our search was a four-year-old link to mental health support from the counseling and students services page. It's completely unacceptable for a district to mention LGBTQ+ people only in the context of mental health crisis. It's up to all members of a school community to hold one another accountable for equitable visibility practices.

Celebrating historically marginalized populations through heritage months and cultural celebrations is one way to affirm the intersectional identities of students at school. LGBTQ+ cultural programming should be comparable to other cultural celebrations in quantity and quality. Celebrating Pride month in June is an opportunity to make your LGBTQ+ students, families, and staff feel seen and valued. Hosting an LGBTQ+ family education night, featuring LGBTQ+ authors and scientists in academic content, and creating displays in school libraries are all wonderful ways to celebrate together. If your school calendar makes celebrating in June difficult, consider having a full month of Pride celebration and programming during a different part of the school year. For a list of days and months observed, celebrated, and honored by the LGBTQ+ community, visit glaad.org/reference/calendar.

Students need to see their identities reflected in all areas of school programming, including curriculum. This book does not discuss lesson plans or curriculum planning, but resources for inclusive curriculum exist across all grade levels. You can find open-source lesson plans and book lists at the following websites:

- Welcoming Schools: welcomingschools.org
- Gender Spectrum: genderspectrum.org
- GSA Network: gsanetwork.org
- GLSEN: glsen.org

The idea of representation across aspects of identity is not a new idea in education circles. I remember examining the idea in Dr. Rudine Sims Bishop's 1990 essay "Windows, Mirrors, and Sliding Glass Doors" in one of my first education classes when I was getting my teaching license. This foundational essay says it's important for all children to see images of themselves and others in the books they read. Today, most educators agree that it is best practice for all students to see their own experiences reflected in the lessons they are taught, while also learning about the experiences of people with other backgrounds and identities.

But what happens when local laws prohibit best practice, or when a school board bans books and discussions about who students are LGBTQ+? The impact of banning best educational practice in schools is student harm. There's no way to sugarcoat this reality. Active harm to students is why so many advocates continue to fight against policies and practices that declare entire populations of students off-limits in education.

If you're an educator working in such circumstances, I encourage you to name this harm when it occurs. Express what you know you should be teaching, and name why you can't. Brainstorm ways you can make valuable content on diverse identities available to students in a community context.

Thank you for being who you are and working where you work. Queer students need educators like you! One affirming adult can be lifesaving for LGBTQ+ students.

Guiding Principles Check-in

Support Happy and Healthy Kids: Happy and healthy kids learn in environments where they see themselves and their identities represented and valued. This concept is not new, but it is new to openly affirm LGBTQ+ people in many school communities. Visible inclusion has a dramatically positive impact on LGBTQ+ kids. Gender Inclusive Schools often receives emails about large numbers of students who make comments to educators during the first two or three days of use of a safe-space poster, sticker, or badge. A small message of recognition and acceptance can be a lifeline for students who have never felt seen before.

Protect Privacy and Confidentiality: Visibility of queer identities, and representation of gender-expansive people, is work that needs to be done proactively. But sometimes when schools take steps to help students feel seen, they inadvertently draw attention to identities students may not wish to disclose or discuss with their peers. Visibility in space and curriculum should not force individual students into the spotlight. Instead, use this proactive education to create meaningful background knowledge about the various kinds of people who exist at school.

Responding to Challenging Questions and Comments

Challenge: *"Why do they need a whole month? Can we celebrate straight kids next month?"*

Response: "Our school celebrates all established cultural heritage and celebration months in similar ways. This helps our community members from historically excluded backgrounds feel seen and welcomed in our schools."

Response: "Heritage and celebration months are meant to proactively address and acknowledge historical discrimination. We will not have a straight pride month because straight people have not been historically or systematically marginalized in our society."

Challenge: *"Schools should be neutral on political issues."*

Response: "Our school does not consider the existence and human rights of our LGBTQ+ community members to be political."

Challenge: *"I don't think it's the school's job to educate students about other people's lifestyles or sex lives. Stop indoctrinating my children."*

Response: "Our education on LGBTQ+ topics does not involve instruction on lifestyles or sexual behaviors. We educate our students on age-appropriate ways to acknowledge and discuss the beautiful diversity of identities that exists in our school community."

Response: "Instruction in our school focuses on tangible behaviors, such as the language people use out loud and how they treat each other. In order to be respectful of our school community members, your child is expected to understand and meet basic behavioral expectations of respect and responsibility."

Challenge: *"Why are we talking about LGBTQ+ topics when these people are such a small percentage of the student population?"*

Response: "Sexual orientation and gender identity or expression (SOGIE) are important topics requiring education because all members of the school community have a sexual orientation, gender identity, and gender expression. Bias toward a particular community, or any aspect of identity, harms all students. It's not a small population; it's everyone."

Response: "Our school community provides targeted services to make sure all populations of students are able to benefit from their public education. Around 3 percent of our students are gender expansive, roughly the same number of students who receive gifted and special education services. When we intentionally plan support for one group of students, it benefits the entire community of learners because all our needs are interconnected."

Review and Reflection

This chapter focuses on the importance of visible support for LGBTQ+ people in school communities. It discusses how to visibly support queer people in schools and the impact of educators' efforts to establish expectations of inclusion. It explains how to equitably plan celebrations and acknowledgments.

After reading this chapter, use the Identity Visibility Reflection form to reflect on your own experiences growing up and to review how various aspects of identity are represented across your school building, district website, social media, other communications, and districtwide practices. Do these representations accurately depict day-to-day life in your school? For example, if 70 percent of your students are students of color, an image on your district homepage that is supposed to represent your student body shouldn't show only White students. If you are completing this form with colleagues, how do your experiences compare with theirs? Are there current practices that come to mind for you that they hadn't noticed, or vice versa? What would the impact be on your school community if inclusive opportunities were realized? What are the next steps necessary to make your aspirations a reality?

Identity Visibility Reflection

This form offers an opportunity to reflect on both the representations of your identities that were present during your school experience growing up and the current visibility and representations of different identities present in your school community today.

Step 1: Examine the various identities listed in the first column of the chart. In the blank spaces, add any additional identities that were part of your life growing up. Think back to your school experiences through grade twelve, and in the second column, check the identities you remember being represented in your own schooling.

Discussion prompts: Did you encounter representations of your identities in curriculum and environment? Were the representations accurate or based on stereotypes? Were your identities discussed? Were some identities held up as the norm?

Step 2: Now think about your students' identities and the climate at your current school. In the third column, check the identities that you've noticed are consistently represented in curriculum and environment. In the fourth column, check the identities that you believe are unrepresented or invisible.

Discussion prompts: If you marked an identity as consistently represented, what is the evidence that you have noticed? If you marked an identity as invisible, what are some ways you could make students who hold these identities feel seen and valued? What barriers to representation exist?

Identities	Represented in Your Own Schooling	Represented in Your Current School	Invisible in Your Current School
Race			
Gender			
Socioeconomic status			
Disability			
Language spoken at home			

→

Identities	Represented in Your Own Schooling	Represented in Your Current School	Invisible in Your Current School
Sexual orientation			
Gender identity			
Religion, spirituality, or lack thereof			
Mental health			
Body size			
Family identity and structure			
Ethnicity			
Cultural practices			
Housing status			

CHAPTER 9

Daily Gender-Inclusive Practices

Systemic supports for gender-expansive students are possible in some school communities and impossible in others. I recognize and uplift educators working in challenging climates, and in this chapter I offer suggestions that can make schools safer for all regardless of the circumstances. If you've ever been in charge of a classroom, you know that individual educators have a great deal of control over the implementation of students' daily education. While the powers that be set the content, educators decide how they communicate with families, how they select and facilitate instructional groupings, and which words they use while teaching. Small choices can have a huge impact. Consider whether you might tweak your teaching practices so that you don't change the content, but present it in a way that allows your gender-expansive students to feel seen and respected.

Gender-Inclusive School Communications

For most families, their child's classroom teachers are their primary point of contact and collaboration with school. When school staff communicate with families, it's best not to make assumptions. Even in communities where the population seems homogeneous, school staff should not presume to know the gender or relationship structure of any family. More than a million LGBTQ+ people in the United States are partners in a same-sex marriage (Williams Institute 2017). Of all LGBTQ+ adults, 29 percent are raising children. Idaho, Utah, Oklahoma, and Arkansas have the highest rates of LGBTQ+ people raising children. (Williams Institue 2019). More than 4 million people have at least one LGBTQ+ parent (Gates 2015). Queer families are everywhere!

Sometimes communities wait for a tipping point for inclusion. When there is enough participation by a particular group, then they change their practices. Inclusion work should be proactive, not reactive. That means thinking ahead about people's needs and planning accordingly.

For example, it may seem as if all the students in your classroom have a mother and father taking care of them at home. If you have been teaching for a long time in this community, the straight, cisgender, two-parent household might be your default assumption. Other types of families might be few or invisible, so sending communications home that ask for a signature by a mother and father might seem perfectly logical and acceptable. However, this language likely isn't acceptable to the other types of families. It suggests that they don't exist or aren't important.

The same communication, with identical content, could be updated in minutes to include all the ways families can be structured, who parents or caregivers are, and their relationships to each other and their children. Listing information options for parent/caregiver 1, parent/caregiver 2, parent/caregiver 3, and parent/caregiver 4 accommodates students living in multigenerational households and students who split their time between multiple homes. Inclusive language lays out a big welcome mat for all the members of your community.

QUEER VOICES

All of my teachers say, "Give this to your parents or guardians" instead of "mom and dad." I have two moms. All families are different.

—Frederick, grade four

Cis/heteronormativity also often appears in school-to-home communications that make assumptions about student identities. For example, one year we received a back-to-school email about drop-off and pick-up procedures. The email began: "When you are dropping off your son or daughter . . . " What about nonbinary or gender-expansive kids for whom the words *son or daughter* don't apply? Does the guidance in the email not apply to them? Are they allowed to be dropped off? Every communication our children receive that standardizes the gender binary makes it harder for people to respect and accept the identities of people who don't fit these false gender norms. Exclusive language and incorrect assumptions harm every member of a school community, because they present false information about the real world.

Find ways to invite sharing of family information that parents and caregivers may want you to know. A great way to start is including on enrollment forms a space where families can share their pronouns. This small step can demonstrate your school community's commitment to inclusion while preventing assumptions and misgendering.

High-Impact Tips for School Communications:

- On school forms, shift toward giving space to list parent/caregiver 1, 2, 3, and 4 instead of mother and father. This change allows for the inclusion of parents and caregivers of all genders, while also respecting students supported by multiple households and extended families.

- In school communications, shift from *son or daughter* and *he or she* to using inclusive words such as *child*, *student*, and singular *they*.

- Do not make cis/heteronormative assumptions about the caring adults in your students' lives. Students are parented by people of all genders with a variety of sexual orientations.

Gender-Neutral Instructional Groupings

Most of the original gender-inclusion policies passed in schools contained language similar to this: *Students will not be separated into instructional groups or placed on teams for activities according to their gender unless there is a compelling pedagogical purpose for doing so.* What schools have found in practice is that there are no "compelling pedagogical purposes" related to student outcomes that support separating students by gender. No evidence suggests that creating a single-gender learning environment makes instruction in schools more academically impactful (Pahlke, Hyde, and Allison 2014). Most gender-based groupings in schools are based on false bias and expectations around stereotypical "girl" and "boy" behavior.

Each time nonbinary students are presented with binary options, they feel a moment of panic over an impossible choice. The options don't include who they are, and this leaves them wondering if they have a place in the world. Nothing is wrong with them. Everything is wrong with pretending that people don't exist outside the binary.

Schools should not be using gender to place students in groups. This applies to lining up, team competitions, field trips, classroom seating charts, or any other activity at school. Other grouping possibilities are endless and take only a few more seconds of effort than saying, "Let's play boys versus girls." No matter where you are teaching, you can take this easy step to create a more gender-inclusive environment for your students.

The most common questions I receive on gender-based student groupings relate to puberty and health education. Most schools I've worked with still separate students into a boys' group and a girls' group for this instruction. This practice results in education that's inaccessible for gender-expansive students and incomplete for all students. It ignores the existence and experiences of gender-expansive students and forces them to either out themselves or learn only about bodies unlike their own. And it deprives all students of comprehensive information about human physiology.

For example, when our daughter was in fifth grade, her school was teaching puberty lessons to a boys' group and a girls' group. We asked administrators where a transgender girl should go to receive accurate information about her body, and they told us that she could go to either group. But neither group provided accurate information about the diverse range of bodies and developmental trajectories experienced by kids of all genders. And it would have been highly stigmatizing for her to be the only girl in the boys' group. It would have been equally harmful for her to sit with the girls and hear that her body was incompatible with her gender. So, we kept her home during the two days of puberty lessons.

It's educational best practice for all students to receive health and puberty instruction together. Ideally, instruction focuses on the proper anatomical words for body parts and explains the impact of anatomy on growth and development without reference to gender stereotypes. For more information on the principles of gender-inclusive puberty and health education, visit the Teaching School Hub website at tshubsfet.org .uk/attachments/download.asp?file=117.

High-Impact Tips for Gender-Neutral Instructional Groupings:

- Group your students in any way other than by body differences.

- Before the school year begins, look at your classroom roster and create several groupings of various sizes, naming them after colors, animals, or whatever you like.

- Interrupt students when they have separated themselves by binary gender and help them reflect on who might feel left out by this approach.

Gender-Inclusive Classroom Language

Phrases such as *boys and girls*, *ladies and gentlemen*, and *brothers and sisters* are so ingrained in North American culture that people say them without a second thought. It's time to pay attention to the real people left out of these phrases. Applying a false gender binary to any group is harmful to those who don't fit the binary, just as masculine-generalized language is harmful to feminine people's experiences. Gender bias and stereotypes hurt everyone.

High-Impact Tips for Gender-Inclusive Language:

- Switch from *ladies and gentlemen* or *boys and girls* to *scholars* or other gender-neutral descriptive terms. Always take into consideration the age and context of the group you are addressing. For ideas, see Gender-Neutral Words for Addressing Groups of Students at the end of this chapter.
- Move from *brothers and sisters* to *siblings*.
- Shift away from *guys* to *folks*, *y'all*, or *everyone*.

Guiding Principles Check-In

Support Happy and Healthy Kids: Being othered, excluded, misrepresented, or diminished can harm anyone's mental health and well-being. Therefore, using accurate language that matches the identities of the people you are communicating with is not only a basic kindness, but also an effective strategy for reducing harm and fostering healthy and happy kids. Kids are more likely to thrive in the company of happy and healthy parents or caregivers. You can contribute to family members' happiness and health by using language that affirms their identities and makes them feel seen and welcome. The effort of carefully selecting words is a small price to pay for increasing the safety of everyone in your school community.

Protect Privacy and Confidentiality: Binary language and practices force gender-expansive people to make a choice: either they must accept a practice or language that excludes them and shoehorn themselves into a category that doesn't reflect who they are, or they must call out the problem and possibly disclose private information before they're ready. For example, if you send a form home for parents and caregivers that requires a signature from "mother or father," you may force a nonbinary parent to lie about their identity or disclose information to you about their gender identity. Likewise, if you group students for a review activity by girls and boys, you may force a nonbinary student to hide who they are or announce publicly that they are neither. By contrast, if you use inclusive language and practices with students and families, you honor the agency of LGBTQ+ people in controlling their private information.

Responding to Challenging Questions and Comments

Challenge: *"Why does this document say "parent/caregiver"? I'm a mom. I've worked hard to be a mom, and it's important to me."*

Response: "When we aren't sure that all adults receiving a document hold the same identities and use the same language, we use inclusive terms that apply to everyone. If your child's teacher knows you use the word *mom* to describe your relationship with your child, that's the language we will use when talking about you specifically."

Challenge: *"I've been greeting my students as 'boys and girls' in the morning for twenty years. I'm not going to change just because of these latest fads."*

Response: "There are many things we used to do as teachers twenty years ago that we no longer do in schools. Kindness isn't a fad, and our expectation is that educators will include everyone at our school."

Challenge: *"Boys and girls are just different. Sometimes, we need to educate them separately so they can focus on learning."*

Response: "The research on single-gender educational environments does not show a measurable benefit in learning outcomes. The harm caused by separating our students by gender outweighs the hypothetical benefit of single-gender education."

Review and Reflection

This chapter discusses tips for being more gender inclusive in your daily classroom practices. It examines strategies for written communication, gender-neutral instructional groupings, and inclusive language used to address groups of students. All these practices are entirely up to an individual educator's discretion. I've never encountered a school community that prohibits inclusive language or requires exclusive language. You can call your students "scholars" instead of "boys and girls" and avoid making assumptions about the adults who care for your students even if your state has passed legislation prohibiting talk of gender or sexual orientation. Be unapologetic in supporting your LGBTQ+ students—especially when the practices have no risk. If you'd like a little practice shifting to gender-inclusive language, see the Gender-Inclusive Language Practice form at the end of this chapter.

Gender-Neutral Words for Addressing Groups of Students

General Terms	Subject-Specific Terms	Fun and Silly Terms
everyone	actors	BUCKAROOS
FOLKS	artists	CHERUBS
FRIENDS	ATHLETES	cool cats
LEADERS	CODERS	crew
learners	historians	EARTHLINGS
people	investigators	epic humans
pupils	mathematicians	FEATHERLESS BIPEDS
scholars	musicians	GOBLINS AND GHOULS
STUDENTS	PERFORMERS	HUMANOIDS
TEAM	READERS	kiddos
tigers (school mascot)	RESEARCHERS	minions
y'all	scientists	party people
	singers	SUNSHINES
	writers	superstars

Gender-Inclusive Language Practice

Review the following language and adjust it to be more gender inclusive.

Dear mother/father: Your son/daughter will be traveling to the science museum next Wednesday. Each student will be required to bring his/her lunch from home.

Good morning, boys and girls (ladies and gentlemen)!

We have an equal number of boys and girls today, so find a partner of the opposite gender to share your notes from today's lecture.

When the boys' restroom pass returns, you may be excused to go.

CHAPTER 10

Gender-Inclusion Policies

This chapter examines the role of an official gender-inclusion policy and its impact on the experiences of LGBTQ+ members of a school community. Such a policy is the responsibility of a school governing board, which is usually composed of individuals elected by their communities. School boards establish and maintain the rules for their schools. School boards have policies on student discipline, curriculum, promotion, graduation, and other situations that require consistency across learning environments. They usually develop policies in consultation with state or provincial school board associations.

Many school districts already have school board policies related to nondiscrimination. But if they haven't been updated in the last five years, the protected classes identified in policy language are likely out of date. For example, the nondiscrimination language may include *sexual orientation* but not *gender identity*.

There is value in establishing and clearly communicating a school community's values even though daily best practices can't be fully detailed in an outward-facing policy. For the same reasons districts have nondiscrimination statements, they should also explicitly state their commitment to protecting gender-expansive students. Antibullying policies that enumerate specific protected classes that are often the targets of discrimination are more effective than policies that do not enumerate the protected classes (Kosciw, Clark, and Menard 2021; Kull et al. 2016; Hatzenbuehler and Keyes 2013). Districts that unapologetically communicate their broad guidelines and protections for gender-expansive students have an easier time implementing best practices in the face of pushback—and protecting the privacy of gender-expansive students. Consider the many examples in which supports for individual trans students have become community controversies. Seemingly overnight, an unwanted spotlight shines on a vulnerable student while their community debates their existence and their rights at school. It's far safer to have these debates directed at policy changes impacting all students than at one student's school experience.

Proactive, public-facing policies also protect school staff who are trying to focus on educating students. If opposition develops, it is directed toward districtwide administrators and school board members instead of educators. Teachers sometimes feel as if they are on their own in defending their LGBTQ+ students. In my professional development sessions, educators often say, "So . . . we have permission to say this? Someone's going to have my back when an angry parent comes in?" Yes and yes—if official districtwide gender-inclusive policies are in place. Communities need to lift the burden of defense from educators and empower them to communicate that gender-expansive kids are valued.

> ### 💬 QUEER VOICES
>
> Our school board passed a gender-inclusion policy last school year. Now everyone feels like: if you don't like it, go to school somewhere else.
>
> —William, grade eleven

Developing a Policy

Most school gender-inclusion policies in the United States and Canada descend directly from the first handful of districtwide policies. Your district doesn't need to reinvent the wheel. It's absolutely okay to adapt policy language used by other school systems rather than start from scratch. When you start from scratch, it's easy to get bogged down in making the policy perfect or unique. This delays adoption and implementation, which in turn delays urgently needed protections. Don't let the perfect be the enemy of the safe.

Policy documents typically begin with a section called Definitions. This section helps readers understand the language in the policy. Some school communities look to their high school GSAs or local LGBTQ+ organizations for help in developing this section. What you define and how you define it should reflect the daily language expectations in your schools. Because language is always evolving, this section should be reviewed regularly to make sure it reflects the language your community members are using to describe themselves and their identities. Wordsmithing the definitions can become contentious and time-consuming. I've seen committees engage in hours of conversations to get the definitions perfect only to have the district communications team make huge changes at the end of the process. Avoid this pitfall by involving all key stakeholders at the beginning of the process, or adopt definitions directly from another school community with a well-written and successful policy.

At the end of this chapter, you will find a model policy created by Gender Inclusive Schools. Feel free to copy or adapt this language to meet your district's needs. The sections included in this policy are ones that Gender Inclusive Schools has found to be most impactful. They also align with the major themes of this book.

Your school community may need to address additional items in your gender-inclusion policy. For example, has your district historically held gendered events, such as Sadie Hawkins dances or powderpuff football games? Does the district have other gendered practices, such as graduation gowns distinguished by binary gender? Gender-inclusion policies should address any issues in a way that makes it easier for all students to focus on learning.

Policy versus Implementation Guidance

Policy language should be broad enough to influence decisions, but flexible enough that support for any student or group of students can respond to specific needs. Prescriptive steps should be housed in internal-facing policy implementation guidance rather than a public-facing policy document. When specific steps are presented to the public, they can become unhelpful or confusing. For example, a gender-inclusion policy should not describe steps employees should take to support students through social transitions. While these steps might be helpful for the school staff doing the supporting, other members of the school community may see them as written in stone if they're part of public-facing policy.

As people are developing policy, they may be tempted to draft language addressing hypothetical scenarios. I encourage policy developers to provide broad language that applies to the vast majority of situations involving gender-expansive students. Outlining what school staff should do if a four-year-old preK student asks to use a new pronoun at school despite having one affirming and one unaffirming parent is outside the scope of policy. While this situation is possible, it's too specific to be addressed in policy because it doesn't reflect the needs of most gender-expansive students.

School board policy is primarily the board director's responsibility. Implementation guidance is a tool district administrators can use to make sure the policy is put into practice. School boards do not usually have expertise requirements for members. School board members may have backgrounds in engineering, medicine, business, or a variety of other fields. It makes sense for school district policy to be an extension of community values, and the implementation of those values to be guided by the professionals responsible for students' day-to-day education.

Many districts handle this separation of policy and implementation guidance by posting their official gender-inclusion policy prominently on their district websites. The implementation guidance is then shared internally with staff. Community members should have access to and be able to ask questions about both policy and implementation guidance. All district documentation in public schools is accessible under the Freedom of Information Act (FOIA).

Hate Speech in Public Comments at School Board Meetings

The public comment portion of school board meetings is used as a platform for hate speech with alarming frequency these days. Most school boards do not respond to each individual providing a public comment, often at the advice of their legal counsel. But public language that causes harm requires an immediate public response to mitigate the damage to the school community. For example, after someone makes a slippery-slope style argument that compares discussion of gender identity in schools to promoting bestiality and pedophilia, it's harmful to just say, "Thank you for your comment," and move on. Silence is complicity. If people are using language at school board meetings that isn't permissible during the school day, it must be called out. This can be a simple statement such as: "While we recognize everyone's right to speak here this evening, we also have an obligation to protect our children and employees. The language used by the last commenter contained speech that was discriminatory to our LGBTQ+ community members and has no place in our schools. Please refer to our district's nondiscrimination policy if you have questions." I've watched LGBTQ+ employees quit their jobs because of language expressed at school board meetings. Saying something—anything—supportive is better than staying silent.

Guiding Principles Check-In

Support Happy and Healthy Kids: Legal guidelines in gender-inclusion policies must be specific to the states or provinces and cities where schools are located. Most state- and provincewide school board organizations now provide their own policy language and legal guidelines related to the support of gender-expansive students. In environments hostile to LGBTQ+ people, the guidelines referenced may directly conflict with educational best practice. I maintain that best practices don't require a popular vote, and human rights shouldn't be up for debate. What's best for happy and healthy students should be the guiding force in school policy.

Protect Privacy and Confidentiality: Forced disclosure language (language that requires school staff to contact a family if their student requests to use a new name or pronoun or seeks any support offered to gender-expansive kids) violates the principle of protecting privacy and confidentiality. It is also discriminatory. If a school district wouldn't automatically contact a student's family when a student is open about their straight or cisgender identity, they should afford the same consideration to queer students. I held my girlfriend's hand in the hallway in high school, and no faculty member called my parents to make sure they knew I was straight. Many students in my graduating class and teachers at my school called me "Davewards," including during instructional class periods. No staff called my house to make sure it was okay to use a name not listed on my birth certificate.

Responding to Challenging Questions and Comments

Challenge: *"I stand with all the people here speaking in opposition to this policy. How can you do something that the majority doesn't want in our schools?"*

Response: "We appreciate you participating in this process by speaking here tonight. There were approximately fifty people speaking in opposition to this policy this evening and fifty people speaking in support. The total number of community members participating at this particular school board meeting is 1 percent of the ten thousand people who voted in the last school board election. The people voting on this policy tonight were elected by majority vote of our entire community. We will not be persuaded at one meeting to veer from best educational practices based on the opinions of 0.5 percent of our community."

Challenge: *"This policy doesn't respect my values, and I don't think I can work at a place that takes such a political stance on social issues."*

Response: "We don't consider the human rights of our students, faculty, and families to be a political matter. We expect our employees to interact with our school communities in ways that do not cause harm. If you are unable to perform your professional responsibilities, then you will be subject to disciplinary action consistent with your bargaining agreement."

Review and Reflection

This chapter discusses how gender-inclusion policies establish behavior expectations in school communities. It looks at the differences between policies and implementation guidelines and explores some common situations that arise during policy development. It also offers language you can use in response to pushback or controversy following the passage of gender-inclusion policies.

Get familiar with your district's current policies. Where are these policies available to the public? How does your district communicate supports for LGBTQ+ or other protected classes of students through policy? When were these policies last updated? After looking at your district's policies, think about next steps. What four or five actions can you take in the coming months to help your policy reflect educational best practice for LGBTQ+ students?

Reviewing your district's policies may be a discouraging activity. If your district's policy has the potential to harm students, what can you do to positively impact the LGBTQ+ people in your school community? Negative circumstances beyond your control can feel overwhelming and hopeless, but the work you do in these environments is important. For example, how can you counteract the negative effects of exclusionary facilities access policies? What positive actions can you take outside school that will help students feel seen and respected?

Model Gender-Inclusion Policy

Introduction

In fulfillment of its mission to _____ (applicable school mission components), _____ (school name) works to provide a school community that is safe for people of all genders. Through policies, practices, curriculum, professional development, parent education, and other programs, _____ (school name) aims to create an informed and affirming environment in which all children develop a healthy self-image and thrive as confident, self-aware learners. Across all settings, teachers and administrators follow our students' lead in acknowledging and affirming the gender that they assert at school.

This document serves as a guide for supporting transgender, nonbinary, and gender expansive students in _____ (school name), but it should be viewed as a starting point for reciprocal collaboration between students, faculty, families/caregivers, and administrators. No two students' needs will ever be the same, and _____ (school name) is committed to tailoring support at school to help each individual be successful. In order to prepare our students to be future leaders, we recognize the importance of increasing cultural competency on topics of gender identity, gender expression, and sexual orientation.

Definitions

The following definitions are not meant to label students, but are intended as functional descriptors.

Gender identity: One's innermost concept of self as male, female, a blend of both, or neither; how individuals perceive themselves and what they call themselves. One's gender identity can be the same as or different from one's sex assigned at birth.

Transgender: Having a gender identity and/or expression different from cultural expectations based on one's sex assigned at birth. The prefix *trans* means "on the other side of."

Cisgender: Having a gender identity that aligns with one's sex assigned at birth. The prefix *cis* means "on the same side of."

Gender binary: The conceptual classification of gender into two distinct forms—male and female—whether by social system, cultural belief, or both simultaneously.

Nonbinary: Not identifying exclusively as a man or a woman. A nonbinary person may identify as both a man and a woman, somewhere in between, or completely outside these categories. Many—but not all—nonbinary people also identify as transgender.

Gender expansive: Having a gender expression, gender identity, and lived experiences that transcend societal expectations for one's sex assigned at birth; often used in research literature to describe people who are not cisgender.

Intersex: An umbrella term for unique variations in reproductive or sex anatomy. Variations may appear in a person's chromosomes, genitals, or internal organs like testes or ovaries. Some intersex traits are identified at birth, while others may not be discovered until puberty or later in life.

Gender-affirming care: Developmentally appropriate care oriented toward understanding and appreciating a person's gender experience. This care consists of an array of services that may include medical, mental health, surgical, and nonmedical services for transgender and nonbinary people. For gender-expansive children, early access to gender-affirming care allows them to focus on their social transition and is crucial to overall health and well-being.

Gender dysphoria: Distress arising from conflict between gender identity and sex assigned at birth.

Gender expression: A person's gender-related appearance and behavior, whether or not stereotypically associated with their assigned sex at birth. People who adopt a presentation that varies from stereotypical gender expectations may describe themselves as gender nonconforming, genderqueer, or gender-fluid.

Gender transition: The process by which some people strive to more closely align their internal knowledge of their gender with their outward expression.

LGBTQ+: Lesbian, gay, bisexual, transgender, queer, plus other identities and orientations. *Plus* refers to the many other terms used by people to describe their gender identity and sexual orientation.

Queer: Having a gender expression, gender identity, or sexual orientation that is not straight and/or cisgender. Sometimes used interchangeably with LGBTQ+. The word *queer* has a derogatory history and associations with violence against LGBTQ+ people. Many LGBTQ+ people have reclaimed this term, but some individuals do not use it to describe who they are because of negative lived experiences and trauma. *Queer* is increasingly being used as a standardized term in educational research.

Sexual orientation: A person's emotional, romantic, sexual attraction to another person based on the gender of the other person. Common terms used to describe sexual orientation include but are not limited to *heterosexual*, *asexual*, *lesbian*, *gay*, and *bisexual*. Sexual orientation and gender identity are different.

SOGIE: Acronym that stands for *sexual orientation and gender identity or expression*, pronounced SO-jee.

Privacy and Confidentiality

All persons, including students, have a right to privacy. This includes keeping a student's actual or perceived gender identity and expression private. Such private information shall be shared only on a need-to-know basis. Students have the right to openly discuss and express their gender identity and expression, and to decide when, with whom, and how much information to share. School personnel may encounter situations where transgender students have not disclosed their transgender status. School personnel must be mindful of the confidentiality and privacy rights of students when communicating with others, so as to not reveal, out, imply, or refer to a student's gender identity or expression.

Names/Pronouns

Using an individual's chosen name and gender-affirming pronouns fosters a safe, supportive, and inclusive environment. _____ (school name) is committed to respectfully using the name and pronouns every member of our community asks us to use. The name and pronouns students use in our community are private and confidential, and will not be shared with third parties without consent. _____ (school name) staff will provide regular opportunities for all students to share information about their names and pronouns, both formally and informally. A "Name Change Request Form" is accessible through our school information systems. While it is expected that inadvertent slips or honest mistakes may occur, _____ (school name) will not tolerate intentional and persistent refusal to respect an individual's gender identity by using the wrong name and/or pronouns.

School Records

_____ (school name) is required by _____ (state law) to maintain records that include the legal names of students and the gender indicated on official government-issued documents. All identifying information related to a student's sex assigned at birth and name/s is considered private medical data. _____ (school name) will not disclose student data information related to gender identity without consent from a student or their legal guardian. For the purpose of supporting gender-expansive students, _____ (school name) distinguishes between a pupil's "official school records" and their "unofficial school records."

Unofficial School Records

Unofficial records include, but are not limited to, report cards, identification badges, classroom rosters, gradebooks, certificates, concert programs, announcements, team rosters, diplomas, and yearbooks. Changes to student names in unofficial records can be made without a court-ordered name change or change to a student's gender marker.

_____ (school name) staff will encourage students to fill out a "Name Change Request Form" to facilitate clear communication of asserted/affirmed names across the school community. However, this form is not required, and should be viewed as optional support. _____ (school name) staff will have open communication with students about the implications of name changes on their school experiences. On unofficial school records, a student's name that differs from the one on their official school records will be listed as "Asserted Name."

Official School Records

A minor child may legally change their name and gender in _____ (state) and other state-level court systems across the United States. Upon receipt of proper evidence

$\longrightarrow$

of the court order, _____ (school name) will exhaustively update all school records to reflect the legal name change. _____ (school name) will retroactively update school records for graduating/former students seeking changes to their transcripts and diplomas.

Facilities Access

All _____ (school name) community members will access facilities (restrooms, dressing rooms, locker rooms, etc.) that correspond to their gender identity. "All Gender" or "Gender Neutral" facilities may be used by any student, regardless of the underlying reason. In any gender-segregated facility, any student requesting increased privacy shall be provided with a safe, non-stigmatizing alternative. However, no student will be required to use a sex-segregated facility that is inconsistent with their gender identity.

Overnight Field Trips and Travel Accommodations

All students at _____ (school name) have the right to participate in overnight field trips and receive travel accommodations in a manner that corresponds to their gender identity. Students are not required to disclose their identity or jeopardize their right to privacy to participate in these opportunities. Students/families seeking increased privacy accommodations will work with school staff to find appropriate solutions that are sensitive to students' needs. _____ (school name) will not facilitate the segregation of any protected class of student, including race, ethnicity, gender, sexual orientation, etc.

Course Enrollment and Academic Instruction

Students shall not be required to take or be denied enrollment in a course on the basis of their gender identity in any educational or academic program. _____ (school name) staff will not use binary definitions of gender to separate students into instructional groupings or as a pedagogical tool for instruction.

→

Athletics

_____ (school name) students will participate in Physical Education and athletics in alignment with their gender identity, and in a manner that is consistent with _____ (state or independent student athletic association) policy.

Student Social Transitions

The term *social transition* refers to the steps an individual may take to bring their external lives into congruence with their internal gender identity. A social transition sometimes, but not always, includes changes in a person's hair, clothing, mannerisms, and other aspects of their gender expression. Social transitions can also include changes to the name and/or pronouns individuals ask us to use. _____ (school name) will not control the timing or manner of a student's decision to socially transition, and will follow the lead of students and families in facilitating necessary communications with the school community. Student social transitions are private and confidential, and information about a social transition will not be disclosed to the larger school community without consent.

Dress Code

All student dress and clothing policies will be gender neutral and _____ (school name) will not enforce any student dress guidelines differently based on gender. When specific dress guidelines exist for concerts, athletics, or formal events, students will choose the items of clothing that align with their gender identity.

Affirming Adults for LGBTQ+ Students

One affirming adult in the life of an LGBTQ+ student can reduce the risk of suicide attempt by 40 percent.[1] _____ (school name) is committed to providing the love, affirmation, and support necessary for all of our students to feel included in our school community. Gender-expansive students can choose to identify and designate a "safe adult" at school who will serve as a resource and support facilitator for concerns related to their inclusion at school.

→

---

1. Trevor Project. 2023. "Acceptance from Adults Is Associated with Lower Rates of Suicide Attempts among LGBTQ Young People." thetrevor project.org/research-briefs/acceptance-from-adults-is-associated-with-lower-rates-of-suicide-attempts-among-lgbtq-young-people-sep-2023.

Curriculum

The guidelines contained in this document are deliberately student focused so that attention can be drawn to the specific procedures and guidelines impacting the daily experiences of gender-expansive students at _____ (school name). However, _____ (school name) is also committed to the full integration and representation of diverse LGBTQ+ identities in our schoolwide curriculum. We know that providing write-in space's (school name) students with windows and mirrors that celebrate the contributions of LGBTQ+ people across all content areas will prepare them to be functioning leaders in a just society.

Staff Professional Development

All employees at _____ (school name) will receive comprehensive professional development and training on best-practices related to the support of gender-expansive community members. This training will be offered at regular intervals and for all new staff and will reflect the evolving understanding of our LGBTQ+ students, staff and families.

Conclusion: Words of Hope and Optimism

In my professional development sessions, one of the norms I set from the beginning is to accept and expect nonclosure as an outcome. It is common for folks to leave my sessions with a significant to-do list of next steps and questions that surfaced during discussion and learning together. The same norm applies to your learning journey here.

There will always be more to do, things you notice to improve, and covert or subtle bias and marginalization to address. Language around gender identity, gender expression, and sexual orientation will continue to evolve. Laws and school policies will too. Equity is a goal to work toward continuously, not a finish line that can ever truly be reached. Depending on your circumstances, reading this book may have felt like affirmation of the wonderful work you are already doing or an exhausting account of goals that seem unattainable for your school community—or maybe something in between. Whatever the case, I'd love to leave you with some words of hope and optimism.

Every act of support and celebration—no matter how small—that you offer to your gender-expansive students is significant. Equity work is lifelong. The decisions you make to increase justice and equity for gender-expansive students in your school community have rippling, far-reaching impacts. Just as the cumulative impact of discrimination can lead to negative school outcomes, the cumulative impact of affirmation and celebration can lead to positive outcomes. Your daily efforts matter—your classroom procedures, your greetings, your meetings with colleagues, the letters you send home, the harmful conversations you shut down, the gaps you fill in other people's knowledge on LGBTQ+ topics, your personal growth and competence, and your visible displays of support. These efforts matter not only to the students who are directly affected in the moment, but also to the students who will walk through the school doors five years in the future.

This may seem like a strange wish from an author, but I hope that this edition of *Gender-Inclusive Schools: How to Affirm and Support Gender-Expansive Students* reads as a historical document in ten years. That schools evolve to the point where this text no longer matches society's acceptance of gender-expansive students and a reframing is needed. That the harmful language in the Responding to Challenging Questions and

Comments sections becomes so taboo that no adult would ever dream of saying such things out loud at school. That the guiding principles of Support Happy and Healthy Kids and Protect Privacy and Confidentiality become ordinary practices taught to every educator. I believe that the adults in school communities have the power to realize these hopes. I'm so excited to support you along the way.

Acknowledgments

This book would not have been possible without the contributions of countless individuals in my life.

Thank you to the Free Spirit Publishing team for your professionalism and assistance throughout the writing, editing, and publishing process. A special thank-you to my editor, Christine Zuchora-Walske, for your unbelievably insightful contributions and suggestions. Your ability to help me identify needs and expand on the content of the text while being patient with me made the book possible. A huge thank-you to Tom Rademacher for asking me to submit a proposal in the first place and for helping me get my ideas structured into a "real book." You're the absolute best!

I am unbelievably grateful for every single educator I've had the opportunity to work with through the Human Rights Campaign Foundation's Welcoming Schools program. Thank you to the Welcoming Schools facilitators for being such incredible role models of how to engage, collaborate, and lead with the educators working every day in schools. Thank you for being thought partners as we constantly refine and reflect on what LGBTQ+ students need. I am in awe of the dedication and commitment you all demonstrate through centering LGBTQ+ young people in this work. Most of all, thank you to Welcoming Schools Senior Director Cheryl Greene for giving me my first opportunity to lead a professional development session on LGBTQ+ topics in 2017. Your mentorship has helped me grow in ways that wouldn't have been possible on my own, and I'm forever grateful for your leadership.

Thank you to my extended family and chosen family. Thank you to my brothers and sisters, Ben, Jess, Kate, and Travis, and their beautiful children, Kai, Aurelia, Simon, and Amelie. Thank you to my in-laws, Rick and Ruth, for caring for my children and showing up at every single event and celebration in our family's advocacy journey. We are so thankful to have all of you in our lives and to have your support, which helps make the work we do as a family possible! Thank you to my chosen family for your unconditional love: Bennett and Lauren, Ashley, Jake and Kate, Greg and Noelle, Ben and Molly, Roxanne, Shimmer, Nomi, Jacob, Pete and Korinne, Gretchen and Hao, Casey, Scott and Richard, Andrea, Ali, Rhamy, Dean and Tom, Zee and Ore, Aliya and Amanda, and Kya. Thank you for helping our family feel safe and supported as we continue to make Minnesota our home.

A huge thank-you to every educator working full-time in schools. The job you do could not possibly be more important. Being a teacher, administrator, office worker, paraprofessional, counselor, social worker, or other school staff member is an awesome responsibility—while also an underappreciated, underpaid, and overworked vocation. I see you and appreciate you for doing your best to make sure students get what they need during the school day and beyond. Thank you for reading this book and for prioritizing the health and happiness of gender-expansive students. Your support is nothing short of life-saving.

Finally, and most importantly, thank you to the gender-expansive students in our schools. Whether or not it's safe for you to be out in your community, existing as your authentic selves is a triumphant act. I hope you can feel the energy, love, and affirmation radiating from the adult allies and queer community members who are doing everything they can to create the school communities you deserve. We love you exactly as you are.

Recommended Resources

Books

Beyond the Gender Binary by Alok Vaid-Menon
In this book, poet Alok Vaid-Menon challenges readers to see gender not in black and white, but in full color. Speaking from their own experience as a gender-expansive artist, they show readers that gender is a creative, changeable form of expression.

Trans Children in Today's Schools by Aidan Key
Key's book helps all members of school communities understand the internal and external variables that a trans child navigates as they explore their gender identity, as well as the challenges experienced by these children and their families, to help readers ensure that all children can count on a safe and welcoming learning environment.

Transgender History: The Roots of Today's Revolution by Susan Stryker
Covering American transgender history from the mid–twentieth century to today, *Transgender History* takes a chronological approach to the subject of transgender history, with each chapter discussing major movements, writings, and events.

Our Gay History in 50 States by Zaylore Stout
Covering all fifty US states plus Washington, DC, and island territories, this book documents the highs and lows of American LGBTQ+ history, reminding readers that LGBTQ+ history is American history.

Websites

Defining LGBTQ+ Terms for Students

welcomingschools.org/resources/definitions-lgbtq-elementary-school

This list can serve as a starting place for educators to respond to questions about LGBTQ+ words from elementary students.

Inclusive Restroom Design Gude

eddesignaward.com/research/wp-content/uploads/2022/02/inclusive-restroom-design.pdf

This comprehensive analysis of gender-specific and inclusive restrooms enumerates key design components of inclusive restrooms.

A Map of Gender Diverse Cultures

pbs.org/independentlens/content/two-spirits_map-html

This interactive map shows and explains how throughout history, cultures around the world have recognized, revered, and integrated more than two genders.

Organizations

Advocates for Youth

advocatesforyouth.org/issue/transgender-young-peoples-health-and-rights

Advocates for Youth works alongside thousands of young people in the United States and around the world as they fight for sexual health, rights, and justice.

AMAZE

amaze.org

AMAZE provides young adolescents around the world with medically accurate, age-appropriate, affirming, and honest sex education they can access directly online, regardless of where they live or attend school.

Gender Inclusive Schools: States with Policy Guidance for Transgender and Gender Diverse Students

genderinclusiveschools.org/gender-inclusion-policy

Gender Inclusive Schools provides parent and educator training to proactively create safe learning environments for LGBTQ+ young people. This page is updated frequently to provide current statewide and provincewide gender-inclusion guidance that reflects best practice in support of gender-expansive students. It includes examples of individual school districts and independent schools guidance.

GSA Network
gsanetwork.org/resources

GSA Network works to strengthen the national movement-building capacity at the intersection of LGBTQ+ youth organizing and racial and gender justice in schools and to develop the next generation of LGBTQ+ leaders, particularly low-income youth and youth of color.

Human Diversity Lab, TransYouth Project
hudl.princeton.edu

The TransYouth Project is the first large-scale, national, longitudinal study of socially transitioned transgender children to date.

PFLAG
pflag.org

Founded in 1973, PFLAG is the first and largest organization dedicated to supporting, educating, and advocating for LGBTQ+ people and their families.

Transforming Families
tffmn.org

Transforming Families is a community where transgender, gender-nonconforming, and questioning youth and their families can come together to support each other in a safe, welcoming space.

Welcoming Schools
welcomingschools.org

For more than fifteen years, the Human Rights Campaign Foundation's Welcoming Schools program has been supporting educators in creating affirming environments for LGBTQ+ students. At this website, you will find a multitude of resources relevant to the support of gender-expansive students, including booklists, lesson plans, and printable PDFs of guidance on best practice. The Welcoming Schools professional development program does an amazing job of viewing the needs of all LGBTQ+ students through an intersectional lens that considers the impact of students with multiple historically marginalized identities. Modules are available in person and online for audiences of all sizes.

References

Bustos, Valeria P., Samyd S. Bustos, Andres Mascaro, Gabriel Del Corral, Antonio J. Forte, Pedro Ciudad, Ester A. Kim, Howard N. Langstein, and Oscar J. Manrique. 2021. "Regret after Gender-Affirmation Surgery: A Systematic Review and Meta-analysis of Prevalence." *Plastic and Reconstructive Surgery Global Open* 9 (3). doi.org/10.1097/GOX.0000000000003477.

Clark, Caitlin M., and Joseph G. Kosciw. 2020. "Engaged or Excluded: LGBTQ Youth's Participation in School Sports and Their Relationship to Psychological Well-Being." *Psychology in the Schools* 59 (1): 95–114. doi.org/10.1002/pits.22500.

Clarke, Kristen. 2023. "The Civil Rights Division Marks the 69th Anniversary of Brown v. Board of Education." US Department of Justice Office of Public Affairs. Updated May 17, 2023. justice.gov/opa/blog/civil-rights-division-marks-69th-anniversary -brown-v-board-education.

Compton, Julie. 2017. "Trans Students Face 'Detrimental' Health Effects without Fed Protection." NBC News. Updated February 25, 2017. nbcnews.com/feature/nbc-out/ without-federal-protections-trans-students-face-potential-health-crisis-n725156.

Domonoske, Camila. 2016. "After 50-Year Legal Struggle, Mississippi School District Ordered to Desegregate." NPR's *The Two-Way*. May 17, 2016. npr.org/sections/ thetwo-way/2016/05/17/478389720/after-50-year-legal-struggle-mississippi -school-district-ordered-to-desegregate.

Gates, Gary J. 2015. "Marriage and Family: LGBT Individuals and Same-Sex Couples." *The Future of Children* 25 (2): 67–87. jstor.org/stable/43581973.

Goldberg, Shoshana K., Ted Lewis, Ellen Kahn, and Ryan Watson. 2023. *2023 LGBTQ+ Youth Report*. Human Rights Campaign Foundation. hrc.im/youthreport2023.

Goldstein, Dana. 2023. "In School Board Elections, Parental Rights Movement Is Dealt Setbacks." *New York Times*. November 11, 2023. nytimes.com/2023/11/08/us/ parental-rights-school-board-elections.html.

Hatzenbuehler, Mark L., and Katherine M. Keyes. 2013. "Inclusive Anti-Bullying Policies and Reducing Risk of Suicide Attempts in Lesbian and Gay Youth." *Journal of Adolescent Health* 53 (1 Suppl): 521–526. doi.org/10.1016/j.jadohealth.2012.08.010.

Henry, Tonya Albert. 2019. "Exclusionary Bathroom Policies Harm Transgender Students." American Medical Association. April 17, 2019. ama-assn.org/delivering-care/ population-care/exclusionary-bathroom-policies-harm-transgender-students.

HRC Foundation. 2023. "Map: Attacks on Gender-Affirming Care by State." Updated November 13, 2023. hrc.org/resources/attacks-on-gender-affirming-care-by-state-map.

Interact. 2021. "Intersex Definitions." Updated February 19, 2021. interactadvocates.org/intersex-definitions.

Kosciw, Joseph G., Caitlin M. Clark, and Leesh Menard. 2021. *The 2021 National School Climate Survey*. GLSEN. glsen.org/sites/default/files/2022-10/NSCS-2021-Full-Report.pdf.

Kull, Ryan M., Emily A. Greytak, Joseph G. Kosciw, and Christian Villenas. 2016. "Effectiveness of School District Antibullying Policies in Improving LGBT Youths' School Climate." *Psychology of Sexual Orientation and Gender Diversity* 3 (4): 407–415. doi.org/10.1037/sgd0000196.

Movement Advancement Project. 2024. "Bans on Transgender People Using Bathrooms and Facilities According to Their Gender Identity." Accessed May 2, 2024. lgbtmap.org/equality-maps/nondiscrimination/bathroom_bans.

Office for Civil Rights (OCR). 2021. "Protecting Students Overview." U.S. Department of Education. Updated January 12, 2023. ed.gov/about/offices/list/ocr/frontpage/pro-students/protectingstudents.html.

Olson, Kristina R., Lily Durwood, Madeleine DeMeules, and Katie A. McLaughlin. 2016. "Mental Health of Transgender Children Who Are Supported in Their Identities." *Pediatrics* 137 (3). doi.org/10.1542/peds.2015-3223.

Olson, Kristina R., Lily Durwood, Rachel Hortion, Natalie M. Gallagher, and Aaron Devor. 2022. "Gender Identity 5 Years after Social Transition." *Pediatrics* 150 (2). doi.org/10.1542/peds.2021-056082.

Pahlke, Erin, Janet Shibley Hyde, and Carlie M. Allison. 2014. "The Effects of Single-Sex Compared with Coeducational Schooling on Students' Performance and Attitudes: A Meta-analysis." *Psychological Bulletin* 140 (4): 1042–1072. doi.org/10.1037/a0035740.

Payne, Marissa. 2017. "Transgender High School Wrestler to Compete against Boys Thanks to New USA Wrestling Policy." *Washington Post*. March 24, 2017. washingtonpost.com/news/early-lead/wp/2017/03/24/transgender-high-school-wrestler-to-compete-against-boys-thanks-to-new-usa-wrestling-policy/.

Price, Myeshia N., and Amy E. Green. 2023. "Association of Gender Identity Acceptance with Fewer Suicide Attempts among Transgender and Nonbinary Youth." *Transgender Health* 8 (1): 56–63. doi.org/10.1089/trgh.2021.0079.

Price-Feeney, Myeshia, Amy E. Green, and Samuel H. Dorison. 2021. "Impact of Bathroom Discrimination on Mental Health among Transgender and Nonbinary Youth." *Journal of Adolescent Health* 68 (6): 1142–1147. doi.org/10.1016/j.jadohealth.2020.11.001.

Rafferty, Jason; Committee on Psychosocial Aspects of Child and Family Health; Committee on Adolescence; Section on Lesbian, Gay, Bisexual, and Transgender Health and Wellness; Michael Yogman; Rebecca Baum; Thresia B. Gambon, et al. 2018. "From the American Academy of Pediatrics | Policy Statement | Ensuring Comprehensive Care and Support for Transgender and Gender-Diverse Children and Adolescents." *Pediatrics* 142 (4). doi.org/10.1542/peds.2018-2162.

Richards, Drew D. 2023. "LGBTQ+ Mental Health and Participation in Sports."
Aperican Psychiatric Association. November 2, 2023. psychiatry.org/News-room/
APA-Blogs/LGBTQ-Participation-in-Sports.

Russell, Stephen T., Amanda M. Pollitt, Gu Li, and Arnold H. Grossman. 2018. "Chosen
Name Use Is Linked to Reduced Depressive Symptoms, Suicidal Ideation, and
Suicidal Behavior Among Transgender Youth." *Journal of Adolescent Health* 63 (4):
503–505. doi.org/10.1016/j.jadohealth.2018.02.003.

Southern Poverty Law Center (SPLC). n.d. "Moms for Liberty." Accessed February 6,
2024. splcenter.org/fighting-hate/extremist-files/group/moms-liberty.

Stanford, Libby. 2024. "New Title IX Rule Has Explicit Ban on Discrimination of
LGBTQ+ Students." *Education Week*. April 19, 2024. edweek.org/policy-politics/
new-title-ix-rule-has-explicit-ban-on-discrimination-of-lgbtq-students/2024/04.

Tanne, Janice Hopkins. 2024. "Nearly Half US States Limit or Ban Access to Gender
Affirming Care for Adolescents, Finds Report." *BMJ 2024* (384): q493. doi.org/
10.1136/bmj.q493.

Thoma, Brian C., Taylor L. Rezeppa, Sophia Choukas-Bradley, Rachel H. Salk, and
Michael P. Marshal. 2021. "Disparities in Childhood Abuse Between Transgender
and Cisgender Adolescents." *Pediatrics* 148 (2). doi.org/10.1542/peds.2020-016907.

Tinker v. Des Moines Independent Community School District. 1969. 393 U.S. 503. 89
S.Ct. 733. 21 L.Ed.2d 731. law.cornell.edu/supremecourt/text/393/503.

Trevor Project. 2020. "Pronouns Usage among LGBTQ Youth." July 29, 2020. thetrevor
project.org/research-briefs/pronouns-usage-among-lgbtq-youth.

Trevor Project. 2023. "Acceptance from Adults Is Associated with Lower Rates of Suicide Attempts among LGBTQ Young People." thetrevorproject.org/research-briefs/
acceptance-from-adults-is-associated-with-lower-rates-of-suicide-attempts-among
-lgbtq-young-people-sep-2023.

Truman, Jennifer L., and Rachel E. Morgan. 2022. "Violent Victimization by Sexual
Orientation and Gender Identity, 2017–2020." Bureau of Justice Statistics. NCJ
304277. bjs.ojp.gov/library/publications/violent-victimization-sexual-orientation
-and-gender-identity-2017-2020.

US Department of Education. 2024. "US Department of Education Releases Final Title
IX Regulations, Providing Vital Protections Against Sex Discrimination." April 19,
2024. ed.gov/news/press-releases/us-department-education-releases-final-title-ix
-regulations-providing-vital-protections-against-sex-discrimination.

Weinhardt, Lance S., Patricia Stevens, Hui Xie, Linda M. Wesp, Steven A. John,
Immaculate Apchemengich, David Kioko, Shannon Chavez-Korell, Katherine M.
Cochran, Jennifer M. Watjen, and Nickolas H. Lambrou. 2017. "Transgender and
Gender Nonconforming Youths' Public Facilities Use and Psychological Well-Being:
A Mixed-Method Study." *Transgender Health* 2 (1): 140–150. doi.org/10.1089/trgh
.2017.0020.

Wernick, Laura J., Alex Kulick, and Matthew Chin. 2017. "Gender Identity Disparities in
Bathroom Safety and Well-Being among High School Students." *Journal of Youth and
Adolescence* 46 (5): 917–930. doi.org/10.1007/s10964-017-0652-1.

Williams Institute. 2017. "Number of Married Same-Sex Couples: On the Two-Year Anniversary of Obergefell v. Hodges." The Williams Institute, UCLA School of Law. June 2017. williamsinstitute.law.ucla.edu/?post_type=publications&p=1609.

Williams Institute. 2019. "LGBT Proportion of Population: United States." The Williams Institute, UCLA School of Law. LGBT Demographic Data Interactive. January 2019. williamsinstitute.law.ucla.edu/visualization/lgbt-stats/?topic=LGBT#density.

Index

on lesson plans, 86
on trans and LGBTQ+ history, 117, 118
organizations, 118–119
websites, 118
restrooms
access to, 49–55
inclusive ones, 52, 118

S

safe learning environments, creation of, 25–26
safe-space language, 84–85
safe-space sticker, 83, 84
safety, as priority, 26
School Social Work Association of America, 15
school traditions, making them welcoming and open to all students, 61
Scout, as queer voice, 67
Sean, as queer voice, 53
sexual orientation
defined, 7
laws prohibiting discussion of, 23
social transition
changing names and pronouns during, 69
communication about, 35–36
defined, 31
experimentation with, 33–34
as individualized; unique, 31
informing peers about, 34–35
as significant moment, 32–33
text about in Model Gender-Inclusion Policy, 110
Society for Adolescent Health and Medicine, 42
SOGIE (sexual orientation and gender identity or expression), 7
Sophia, as queer voice, 22
sports
text about in Model Gender-Inclusion Policy, 110
TGD youth's participation in, 59–61
Sports and Gender (form), 65, 66
standardized responses
to challenging questions and comments, 21–27

examples of, 24–25
form for, 28, 29
Student Information Sheet (form), 69–70, 75
student leadership, and gender inclusion, 62–63
support, importance of visible support, 83–86

T

Teaching School Hub (website), 94
Title IX, school sports participation and, 60
traditions, making school traditions welcoming and open to all students, 61
transgender
defined, 6
statistic about, 41
transgender and gender-diverse (TGD) youth
case for access to gender-affirming care for, 41, 42
discrimination against, 41
health-care needs of, 40–42
support for, 43–44
travel accommodations, text about in Model Gender-Inclusion Policy, 109

U

urinary tract infections, trans kids as at increased risk for, 50

V

visibility
equitable visibility, 85–86
of inclusivity in physical spaces, 83–84

W

Welcoming Schools (website), 86, 119
William, as queer voice, 100
"Windows, Mirrors, and Sliding Glass Doors" (Bishop), 86
World Professional Association for Transgender Health, 42–43
Wren, as queer voice, 59

Digital Resources

A fillable PDF of each form is available on TCM Content Cloud.

Accessing the Digital Resources

The digital resources can be downloaded by following these steps:

1. Go to www.tcmpub.com/digital
2. Use the 13-digit ISBN number to redeem the digital resources.
3. Respond to the question using the book.
4. Follow the prompts on the Content Cloud website to sign in or create a new account.
5. The content redeemed will appear on your My Content screen. Click on the product to look through the digital resources. All file resources are available for download. Select files can be previewed, opened, and shared. Any web-based content, such as videos, links, or interactive text, can be viewed and used in the browser but is not available for download.

For questions and assistance with your ISBN redemption, please contact Teacher Created Materials.

email: customerservice@tcmpub.com
phone: 800-858-7339

About the Author

Dave Edwards is a queer person and career educator who has served in almost every role in preK–12 school communities: special education paraprofessional, special education teacher, middle and high school classroom teacher, special education coordinator, dean of students, and assistant head of school. Dave was lead instructor for the nontraditional teacher licensure program in emotional and behavioral disorders at the University of Minnesota–Twin Cities and a professor in the teacher preparation program at Hamline University before devoting his efforts full-time to Gender Inclusive Schools. Dave is the proud parent to a transgender daughter. The discrimination she experienced in kindergarten led to his vocation of helping school communities create safe learning environments, which in turn informs *Gender-Inclusive Schools: How to Affirm and Support Gender-Expansive Students*. He serves on the board of the Minnesota Transgender Health Coalition, and his family is heavily involved with Transforming Families Minnesota. Dave has been quoted by the *New York Times*, *Rolling Stone*, NBC News, and *Into*. He lives in the Twin Cities, Minnesota, area.